Marketing in Europe
Case Studies

Community of
European
Management
Schools

EUROPEAN MANAGEMENT SERIES

The European Management Series derives from a unique collaboration, the Community of European Management Schools (CEMS), which was formed in 1988 and integrates both academic and corporate members. Together they develop and disseminate a shared body of European knowledge in the field of management and award the CEMS Master's degree.

With particular emphasis upon meeting the needs of management students for high-quality European-based material, the series aims to bring to international management education a strongly European perspective. Prepared by CEMS faculty, it includes textbooks, case studies and other volumes that examine key European and international management issues.

Marketing in Europe

Case Studies

edited by
Jordi Montaña

Sage Publications
London • Thousand Oaks • New Delhi

Introduction and editorial arrangement © Jordi Montaña 1994
Chapters 1 and 2 © Guillermo Cisneros and Jordi Montaña 1994
Chapter 3 © Jordi Montaña and Maria José Trell 1994
Chapter 4 © Michele Costabile and Maria Carmela Ostillio with Enrico Valdani 1994
Chapter 5 © Bernard Dubois, Joachim Malato de Sousa and Eduardo Cruz 1994
Chapter 6 © Ron J.H. Meyer and Ad T. Pruyn 1994
Chapter 7 © Jean-Jacques Lambin 1994
Chapter 8 © Wolfgang Breuer and Richard Köhler 1994
Chapter 9 © Helmut J. Kurz 1994
Chapter 10 © Jesper Christiansen and Kenneth Nielsen 1994
Chapter 11 © Josef A. Mazanec 1994

First published 1994

SAGE Publications Ltd
6 Bonhill Street
London EC2A 4PU

SAGE Publications Inc
2455 Teller Road
Thousand Oaks, California 91320

SAGE Publications India Pvt Ltd
32, M-Block Market
Greater Kailash – I
New Delhi 110 048

British Library Cataloguing in Publication data

Marketing in Europe: Case Studies. –
(European Management Series)
  I. Montaña, Jordi II. Series
  658.8

  ISBN 0–8039–8955–5
  ISBN 0–8039–8956–3 pbk

Library of Congress catalog card number 93–86496

Typeset by Mayhew Typesetting, Rhayader, Powys
Printed in Great Britain by The Cromwell Press Ltd,
Broughton Gifford, Melksham, Wiltshire

Contents

The Contributors

Wolfgang Breuer and Richard Köhler
Universität zu Köln, Germany

Jesper Christiansen and Kenneth Nielsen
Copenhagen Business School, Copenhagen, Denmark

Guillermo Cisneros, Jordi Montaña and Maria José Trell
ESADE (Escuela Superior de Administración y Dirección de Empresas),
Barcelona, Spain

Michele Costabile
Università di Calabria, Cosenza and Università Commerciale Luigi
Bocconi, Milan, Italy

Eduardo Cruz
CIFAG (Centro de Informação, Formação e Aperfeiçoamento em
Gestão), Sintra, Portugal

Bernard Dubois
Group HEC (Hautes Etudes Commerciales), Jouy-en-Josas, France

Helmut J. Kurz
Wirtschaftsuniversität Wien, Austria

Jean-Jacques Lambin
Université Catholique de Louvain, Louvain-la-Neuve, Belgium

Joachim Malato de Souza
Ibermarketing, Lisbon, Portugal

Josef A. Mazanec
Wirtschaftsuniversität Wien, Austria

Ron J.H. Meyer and Ad T. Pruyn
Rotterdam School of Management, Erasmus University, Rotterdam,
the Netherlands

Maria Carmela Ostillio and Enrico Valdani
Università Commerciale Luigi Bocconi, Milan, Italy

Acknowledgements

A pan-European book like this would not have been possible without the collaboration of a large number of people. I wish to thank not only the authors of the cases, but also all the members of the Community of European Management Schools (CEMS) Interfaculty Group on Marketing: Professors Renato Fiocca of the Università Commerciale Luigi Bocconi; Hanne Hartvig Larsen of the Copenhagen Business School; Ad Pruyn of Erasmus Universiteit Rotterdam; Carlo Gallucci of Escuela Superior de Administración y Dirección de Empresas (ESADE); Bernard Dubois of the Group HEC (Hautes Etudes Commerciales); Richard Köhler of the Universität zu Köln; Celia Phillips of the London School of Economics; Jean-Jacques Lambin of the Université Catholique de Louvain; Sigurd V. Troye of the Norwegian School of Economics and Business Administration, Bergen; Christian Belz of Hochschule St Gallen; Lars-Gunnar Mattsson of the Stockholm School of Economics; and Josef Mazanec of the Wirtschaftsuniversität Wien; all of whom spent a great many hours discussing the approach and content of this first book.

I would also like to thank Nicole de Fontaines for her assistance in arranging for the book's publication; Antonia Maria Serra and Cinta Fernández of ESADE's International Academic Relations Service for their help in co-ordinating the project; Josep Franch of ESADE's Department of Marketing Management and Research Assistant Loreto Rubio for their work in checking facts and obtaining background information; Patricia Matthews for translating the Spanish cases; and Dr Mike Saren of the University of Bath for his invaluable comments on the manuscript.

There are no doubt a number of people at all the CEMS schools who helped in preparing the cases that make up this book. Although I do not know all of them by name, I would like them to know that their work is very much appreciated.

And last, but not least, I would like to thank the restaurants Set Portes in Barcelona, Burgundy auf de Maes in Rotterdam and Tivoli Park in Copenhagen and a legion of taxi drivers in Paris and Milan who provided the settings for many of our meetings.

Jordi Montaña
Chair of the CEMS
Interfaculty Group on Marketing

Introduction

Jordi Montaña

This is a book about marketing, international marketing and European marketing, in that order. In other words, it is first and foremost a textbook that covers the key features of marketing. The various cases analyse some of the decisions businesses make when marketing their products, services and brands: decisions on new product strategies, pricing, distribution, sales networks, advertising and promotion – in short, issues that are part of the corporate marketing mix.

Some of the cases deal with specific issues and illustrate how a marketing plan can reveal whether or not a particular marketing mix is coherent. Other cases examine marketing strategies, market research and market segmentation, and analyse decisions that involve selecting target segments and positioning products, brands, events, cities and countries.

The book looks at international marketing, examining the different steps involved in going international: defining growth strategies in terms of objectives vis-à-vis products, markets and countries; designing an entry strategy and deciding whether it is better to break into the market directly or through exports, joint ventures or some other type of co-operative arrangement. Some of the cases deal specifically with the problems of small businesses, whose attempts to go international are likely to be less formal than those of their larger counterparts.

And lastly, this is a book about Europe. Some cases deal with companies that are internationalizing by developing marketing plans for one or more European countries, or strategies aimed at maintaining or improving their initial position in these markets. Other cases are in-depth studies of business operations in some specific country. All these cases underscore the fact that Europe is now a huge single market with tremendous potential for short-term growth, but also a market made up of many tremendously different small markets, which provide considerable opportunities but also pose a great number of marketing problems. In order to make the most efficient use of available marketing resources, we need more and more complete information about this complex and variegated unit known as Europe. It is our hope that this book will help supply this information.

We could not have even begun to meet such ambitious aims had this book not been a co-operative project. It is the result of studies carried out by members of the CEMS Interfaculty Group on Marketing and marketing faculty members of a number of the CEMS member schools. CEMS (the Community of European Management Schools) was founded in 1988 with the aim of training future Euromanagers by defining a common body of knowledge and management experience leading to the CEMS Master, a common degree awarded to candidates from the various member schools. This degree programme has stimulated increased co-operation between schools as interfaculty groups from each of the functional areas work together to design curricula that are more distinctly European in content, promote student and faculty exchanges, undertake joint research and create teaching material, of which *Marketing in Europe* is an example.

Marketing in Europe presents eleven cases that illustrate a variety of marketing situations and the way they have been handled by certain businesses and organizations.

Moët & Chandon (two cases, A and B)

Moët & Chandon is a well-known producer of champagne operating throughout the world. The first part of Case A explains how champagne is produced and describes the strict regulations governing use of the name Champagne. It then goes on to study company performance and the breakdown of Moët & Chandon's international sales, with special emphasis on the European market and an analysis of market behaviour in different European countries. But the real aim of the case is to encourage readers to think about the different strategies of growth open to a company whose main product can only be produced in limited amounts despite the fact that demand is increasing. Case discussion should revolve around growth strategies and possible product/market combinations based on an analysis of the company's operating environment, existing threats and opportunities, and the strengths and weaknesses of the Moët & Chandon Group.

Moët & Chandon Case B describes how the company implemented one of the possible growth strategies and began producing a sparkling wine (*cava*) in Spain. This involved creating a new product and brand that would profit from the company's international reputation without stealing sales from its flagship product: French champagne. The case analyses the Spanish market and Spanish consumer behaviour, setting the stage for a discussion on new product development, selecting markets, defining the product concept, brand positioning and subsequently defining the international marketing strategy.

SEAT

SEAT is a Spanish automobile manufacturer that now belongs to the Volkswagen–Audi Group, although it is managed directly from Spain. Up until 1980 the company had produced automobiles under licence from Fiat, largely for sale on the domestic market. When Fiat pulled out, the company's prospects were poor. Its only chance to survive was to export; these days domestic sales alone are not enough for any automobile manufacturer. As SEAT's sales manager explains, the company had to decide what markets to enter, as an unknown company from a country with little or no reputation as an automobile manufacturer. They had to make SEAT an attractive option in an industry where competition is particularly fierce, and they had to do this fast.

This case provides an opportunity to study market selection and entry strategies, particularly for Europe.

Nescafé Italy

This case provides an opportunity to compare Italy with other coffee-drinking countries and examines the need for a new marketing strategy and detailed marketing plan for Nescafé, an instant coffee produced by the Swiss firm Nestlé, which has been available on the Italian market for over thirty years. The case analyses the Italian market and the strategy used to position the product from the time it entered the market in 1962 until the present day, when a decision must be made as to whether the company should give up its position in the instant coffee market niche or embark on a drive to become its absolute leader.

Dulato

The Dulato case is set in Portugal and presents a typical problem involving a company's sales force. Dulato operates in the food and beverage industry and has over twenty sales representatives working throughout the country. The sales manager's resignation forces the company to face up to a number of organizational problems. The case deals with the most important aspects of sales management, including the distinction between company and freelance sales representatives, sales network objectives, remuneration systems and how to define and organize sales territories. The Dulato case provides a good opportunity to discuss the particular characteristics of sales operations in Portugal and compare them with readers' own countries.

Nico Duin BV

Nobody questions the fact that business needs to go international. There are numerous examples of big businesses that have expanded their operations throughout Europe, but there are far fewer cases of small businesses that have taken the plunge. Nico Duin BV, a small Dutch company that manufactures machinery for processing wood components for the construction industry, is one of them.

Nico Duin was planning to move into the German market and this case examines the importance of the company owner's motivation to embark on an internationalization process. Not much has been written about this in international marketing literature but it is a key factor in small and medium-sized business decisions. Looking for new markets abroad is often more a personal decision on the part of the boss than a matter of competitive pressure as it is in the case of big businesses.

This chapter also examines some of the problems that face small businesses: lack of information and/or time to acquire it, resource shortages and the consequent constraints on the ways these companies can enter the markets of their choice.

Volvo Trucks Europe

The Volvo case provides a good background for discussing the problems of an international company with a multinational marketing organization and clearly illustrates the dilemma posed by attempts to 'think globally and act locally' in the context of the Single European Market. It also illustrates the importance of international segmentation as a prerequisite for developing an international marketing strategy.

The prospect of the Single European Market meant that Volvo Europe had to co-ordinate the different marketing strategies applied by its organizations in the various EC countries. At the time the case was written Volvo had a marketing system whereby each country was treated as a domestic market: sales were made through importers and dealers in each country; prices of vehicles, components and service differed from one country to another, depending on local competition; and service contracts for products purchased in one country were not necessarily valid in another. Advertising and promotion were co-ordinated only to the extent of ensuring that the Volvo brand and logotype always had the same look. Moreover, European production planning was based on sales forecasts from each of the national importers and had proven to be fairly inaccurate as well as increasing production costs. Under these circumstances Volvo's management had to decide what elements of their marketing mix should be standardized for all of Europe, and to what extent.

Procter & Gamble

The world's leading manufacturers of consumer products are finding that, although Europe is a very attractive market because of its high standards of living, it actually consists of a large number of relatively small markets with enormous cultural differences. These companies therefore need to find the right balance between global marketing, European marketing and local marketing. This is illustrated in the Procter & Gamble case, which deals with the introduction of a new product: a combined shampoo/hair conditioner based on BC-18 technology. This product was successfully introduced on the US market under the name Pert Plus and the company subsequently decided to introduce it in Europe, starting with Germany, Great Britain, France, Scandinavia and the Benelux countries.

The case demonstrates the problems involved in designing European marketing strategies and plans, and deals specifically with the issue of choosing a name for the product, comparing the different advantages and disadvantages involved in adopting pan-European or local branding.

Export Advertising Strategies

The case discusses the design of an advertising strategy for a product that is to be marketed internationally using country-of-origin effects. The case suggests using an Austrian product and provides material that will enable readers to develop advertising strategies for such a product in particular countries. It addresses various factors that should be taken into account, such as the images of different countries, the impact of stereotypical country images used in the European market, and how to define a European advertising strategy.

Copenhagen – City of Culture 1996

This chapter deals with an entirely different set of circumstances. Every year one EC city is chosen to be the City of Culture. In 1996 it will be Copenhagen's turn, giving the city a chance to be a cultural showcase for the rest of Europe, boosting tourism and spurring economic and business activity. A number of different agents will be affected and both they and their objectives must be identified. The case addresses the need to determine which interest parties will be involved, and define their main objectives. In addition, it asks for a plan for marketing the City of Culture in both Denmark and the other EC countries.

International Tourism Marketing

This case discusses the approach to marketing that a National Tourist Office (NTO) might adopt, taking Austria as an example. The NTO regards other countries both as markets which can supply Austria with tourists and as destinations which can compete with Austria for these same tourists. The case considers how the growth share matrix, which is commonly used in designing market strategies for products, can also be applied to services. A number of tourism-generating countries are rated in terms of the potential size of their markets, the growth rate of these markets and their shares of the tourist market. The case offers a new perspective on the European market which will be of interest to everyone involved in marketing services in general and tourism in particular.

As you can see, the hallmark of this book is diversity. It includes cases about large organizations and small businesses; about consumer products, industrial goods and services; about marketing cities and countries. It is diverse too in the problems it addresses: international strategy, marketing strategies, launching new products, brand problems, managing sales networks, advertising – in short, virtually all the problems that require marketing decisions. And lastly, it is diverse in the countries and situations it describes – a reflection of the European diversity that is characteristic of our Interfaculty Group on Marketing.

1

Moët & Chandon A
The problem of growth

Guillermo Cisneros and Jordi Montaña

This case considers the situation of a company operating in a sector with strict regulations governing production of its star product. The production of sparkling wine, particularly champagne, is limited not only by regulations on the production method but also by regulations setting a production maximum and restricting the use of brand names for other types of beverages. These restrictions are intended to ensure the quality of the final product.

The problem facing Moët & Chandon in this case is that while there is increasing worldwide demand for Moët & Chandon, production restrictions prevent the company from meeting this demand. The company is already a leader and virtually dominates the market. How therefore is Moët & Chandon to design appropriate growth strategies in this context?

In 1987, following a mild but rainy spring in the Champagne district of France, humidity increased considerably and it remained damp for several weeks – right until the end of June. The dampness caused the grape leaves and stocks to start rotting on the vine even before the blooming season, which had been expected in the month of May. But at the end of June there was a spectacular change in the weather: the temperatures soared, the sun shone brightly and the vines blossomed perfectly, free from attacks by parasites and with the rot in remittance thanks to good weather and adequate care. The ratio of grapes to blossoms was exceptional, and picking, scheduled for one hundred days after blooming, began in early October.

Weather, however, is not the only thing that threatens champagne production every year.

The wine of Champagne

Vines have been growing in Champagne since the beginning of Christianity. As far back as the sixteenth century the red and rosé wines from the Champagne district were much appreciated by the courts of the French kings.

The sparkling wine of champagne originated with Dom Pérignon (1639–1715), bursar and master of the wine cellars at the Benedictine Abbey of Hautvillers:

- A grower, Dom Pérignon studied how certain types of vine acclimatized to the soil.
- A wine taster, he defined and demonstrated how to blend different wines to achieve one great Champagne wine.
- A cellar master and oenologist, he discovered sparkling wine and first used cork stoppers to conserve its sparkling property as well as the very quality of the wines that give the products of the Champagne district their quality and reputation (see Appendix 1).

Champagne began to be sold commercially in the eighteenth century with the development of new techniques for controlling the wine's sparkling properties and the advent of more resistant bottles, which made it possible to reduce what had formerly been a very high rate of bursts.

The vines of Champagne

The vines cover the cliffs above the Ile de France region, at a height of 150–200 metres above sea level. The subsoil is a chalk known as Belimnita quadrata (from the Senonian stage of the Upper Cretaceous period), which drains the excess water and yields it up again during the dry summers. The climate of Champagne represents a transition between the dominant oceanic influences of the Parisian Basin and continental tendencies from the east.

'Champagne' is an *appellation contrôlée* which can be used only by wines produced in that particular zone from a certain type of vine. Production is limited; the wine must be produced according to the traditional procedure which includes secondary fermentation while in the bottle, and a series of other local traditions must also be observed.

The Champagne district was delimited by law on 22 July 1927. It extends over 35,000 hectares, 26,700 of which are currently under cultivation. Annual production amounts to between 600,000 and 800,000 *pièces* of 205 litres each, or the equivalent of between 164 and 219 million bottles (see Appendix 2). Approximately 80% of the vines are situated in the Department of the Marne, on the slopes of the Reims Mountain, in the Marne River valley and the Côte des Blancs. Approximately 5% of the vines are planted in the Department of Aisne and another 15% in the Aube.

The traditional vines of Champagne

The three traditional vines of Champagne are as follows:

- Black grapes account for 72% of the crop: the Pinot Noir variety, planted on the slopes of the Reims Mountain, in the upper Marne River valley and in the Department of the Aube; the Pinot Meunier variety, planted in the Marne River valley and the Department of Aisne.
- The remaining 28% of the grapes are the white Chardonnay variety which is planted in Côte des Blancs.

The vines are thickly planted (7,000–10,000 plants per hectare). They are carefully trained and regularly pruned. All this limits the strength of the vines and, naturally, their production, but assures that the grapes will be of the highest quality. The maximum production of champagne is decided upon each year by the CIVC (Comité Interprofessionnel du Vin de Champagne) in accordance with the conditions of that particular year and the quality of the harvest. However, no more than 13,000 kg of grapes per hectare may be designated *appellation contrôlée*.

In 1987 the maximum yield per hectare was set at 13,500 kg of grapes (100 litres for every 150 kg of grapes) or 43 hectolitres of wine *AOC* (*appellation d'origine contrôlée*) champagne per hectare.

A ranking of the vines in the Champagne district assigns each vineyard a value, which ranges from 80% for the simpler wines to 100% for the *grandes cuvées*. This enables the CIVC to set the price per kg of grapes before picking starts, basing its calculations on the figure set for the wines classified as 100%. The vineyards valued at 100% are:

- Ambonnay, Ay, Beaumont, Bouzy, Louvois, Mailly, Puisieulx, Sillery, Tours-sur-Marne, Verzay and Verzenay for black grapes; and
- Avize, Chouilly, Cramant, Le Mesnil, Oger and Oiry for white grapes.

How champagne is made

Grape supplies At harvest time supplies are obtained in the form of either grapes from the vintner's own vines or must from grapes purchased elsewhere. Grapes purchased during the harvest season are pressed at the vineyard before being shipped in cistern trucks to the vintner's. During the rest of the year clear wines are purchased from the growers and their co-operatives.

Pressing Grape pressing in Champagne is regulated as follows: 4,000 kg of whole, healthy, saleable grapes are pressed separately to obtain 2,050 litres of vintage wine, 410 litres of *première taille* and 205 litres of deuxième taille – which are entitled to be called champagne. The rest are sent to the distillery where they are used to produce *marc de champagne* (a strong brandy). The yield for champagne grapes is 66.6% (150 kg of grapes give 100 litres of must).

Each grower's grapes are pressed separately, and juices of the same vintage are fermented separately. Wines from different vineyards are blended only after sampling the preliminary blends.

Fermentation Fermentation takes place in stainless-steel vats at controlled temperatures of between 18 and 20°C. Selected yeasts are used in the process, which lasts one to two weeks.

Malo-lactic fermentation Malic acid is transformed to lactic acid, which makes it possible to reduce the natural acidity of the wine and obtain lighter, better-balanced wines. Great care must be taken in pressing the grapes and handling the alcohol and malo-lactic fermentation processes if high-quality wines are to be produced.

Racking Once the alcohol and malo-lactic fermentation processes are complete, the wines are allowed to cool gradually. They are racked and spun by centrifugal force in order to speed up the clarification process and keep the wines clean. The wines are then stored at a temperature of about 10°C.

Blending, preliminary blends, final blends The contents of all the vats are systematically tested and analysed in order to obtain preliminary blends of wines, which vary in quality and volume depending on the year they were produced. These preliminary blends are stored for one year. The final blends of the various vintages are decided upon after sampling the preliminary blends and testing trial formulas. Numerous tasting sessions are held in order to alter and compare the different formulas before making a definite decision. Already blended young wines are further blended with certain qualities of older wine in order to obtain the right proportions.

Bottling The wine is then bottled, and effervescence produced in the cellar. The bottled wine is a mixture that has previously been cold-stabilized at low temperature (−3°C), sweetened with sugar at the rate of 24 grams per litre and racked by isinglass, and to which selected laboratory-cultivated yeasts have been added, along with binding agents (fish glue, tannin, bentonite or alginate).

Second fermentation, producing effervescence The bottles are placed in a horizontal position. The action of the yeast ferments the alcohol a second time, producing the effervescence in the champagne. The temperatures in the cellars are kept between 12 and 13°C, and fermentation takes six to eight weeks.

Ageing in the wine cellars The length of time the bottles are aged depends upon the vintage: two years for non-vintage *cuvées*, three to five for vintage champagnes and over five years for special *cuvées*. This lengthy ageing process, with the bottles in a horizontal position and kept at constant temperature in the cellars, is essential to the quality and purity of the champagne. During the ageing process there are numerous reactions between the dead yeasts and the wine. The time factor is of prime importance at this stage of production.

Remuage As effervescence is produced, a sediment is also formed. The wine must be clarified in its bottle. This is done by working down the sediment until it nearly covers the cork. The bottles are placed neck downwards in *pupitres* and given a slight turn every day for five to six weeks.

Dégorgement Once the bottle has reached a perpendicular position, the wine in the neck of the bottle is frozen at a temperature of $-28°C$, thus permitting the easy extraction of the sediment-coated cork. Prior to final bottling the *liqueur d'expédition* is added so as to impart any of the degrees of dryness of flavour (*brut, extra-dry, sec, demi-sec*) required by the vintage and the taste preferences of the countries for which it is destined. The bottle is finally corked and wired, labelled and packed for shipping (see Appendix 2 for labelling regulations).

Quality control Throughout the entire production process, from the moment the grapes and must are delivered until the bottles are sent on their way, the laboratory continually analyses and tests the wine, carrying out the controls necessary to assure the highest quality.

The quality and evolution of the different vintages are monitored by means of regular tastings.

Champagne regulations and restrictions

Use of the name Champagne

Use of the name Champagne is regulated by a large number of articles contained in the Statute of Champagne Winegrowers. The French tax authority, the National Institute of *Appellations d'Origine* (INAO), the Interprofessional Committee for Champagne Wine (CIVC), the revenue services, the fraud brigade and numerous other agencies perform a watchdog function, seeing that the statute is adhered to and the regulations on *appellations d'origine* are enforced.

Beginning in the early twentieth century a series of laws were passed, defining the *appellation d'origine* Champagne. Chief among them are the laws and decrees of 1919, 1927, 1935 and 1938, which:

- establish the boundaries of the Champagne growing and production region;
- designate the only authorized vines (currently Pinot Noir, Pinot Meunier, Chardonnay);
- establish rules on transporting grapes and wines destined to produce champagne;
- prohibit manufacture in the Champagne district of any sparkling wine not produced from grapes harvested in the Champagne growing region;
- set the maximum yield per hectare of producing vines;
- set the minimum alcoholic content of the must obtained from the vintage;
- set the desired yield from pressing, within the limit of one hectolitre for every 150 kg of grapes;
- limit the right to use the name Champagne to 98.50% of the wines produced;
- establish that the wine must be bottled in the district where it was produced;
- stipulate that the wine must be aged in the bottle for a minimum of one year prior to being shipped from the vintner's;
- stipulate that the wine may be sold only in bottles;
- establish regulations for planting, handling and pruning the vines.

During recent years many complementary measures have been enacted in order to define production conditions precisely and provide solid guarantees of origin. The prime purpose of these measures is to improve the quality of champagne even further. Among the most recent measures enacted are the following:

- Analysis and sampling of the vintages after effervescence is produced are compulsory for all aspirants to the *appellation d'origine* Champagne.
- Bottling any wine of *appellation d'origine* Champagne before 1 January of the year following its harvest is strictly prohibited.
- Use of certain types of wine presses is prohibited. Use of all wine presses with a capacity of under 2,000 kg will be discontinued in the near future.

The Châlons Commission and the CIVC

The Decree-Law of 28 September 1935 created the Châlons Commission, which in 1941 became the CIVC (Comité Interprofessionnel du Vin de Champagne), a semi-public agency made up of representatives of the growers and shippers.

There are two presidents at the summit of the CIVC: the growers' president and the shippers' president. Final decisions are reached by consensus. A representative of the French government, in this case the *préfet*, ratifies these decisions. Nevertheless, the CIVC is completely autonomous and politically independent. The two presidents are advised by a permanent commission, also made up evenly of growers' and shippers' representatives. This commission works directly with twelve subcommittees, each of which is in charge of some particular aspect of champagne production or marketing. Members of the commission and subcommittees are democratically elected by the shippers' and growers' associations.

The CIVC has broad powers in relation to the following:

Defence and promotion of the appellation Champagne Champagne is probably the world's most imitated product in the food and beverage industry – and probably the best known. The commission therefore has well-oiled legal machinery in charge of defending champagne against any abuse of its name or image. According to Alex du Réau, the director of the CIVC, there is about one case of this per week. Attempts have been made to baptize almost everything from mineral water to cigarettes and toilet paper with the name Champagne. Naturally enough, there have been constant attempts in France and elsewhere to use the name to designate sparkling wines.

Recently the EC decided that as of 1992 even the use of the words *méthode champenoise* on labels of sparkling wines not produced in the Champagne district would be prohibited: 'In any case, ideas are changing somewhat and producers of high-quality sparkling wines from other parts of France and elsewhere in the world are now more interested in emphasizing the intrinsic value of their products. The Spanish case is exemplary and now the word cava is recognized everywhere'. Alex du Réau concedes that the Italians, New Zealanders and some California vintners are also beginning to think along these lines. He also declares that communication accounts for 40% of the CIVC's annual budget.

Organization and control of production; distribution of raw materials in accordance with the terms of the inter-trade contract; and monitoring the harvesting process to assure that it is correct Here a key function is to set the price of grapes, which has remained stable for the past seven years even though overall production varies on a scale of 1–5 depending on the year. In 1987 the price of grapes was 21.77 francs per kg for those from the best, or 100% vineyards (see Appendix 3). Since 1956 production has increased from 30 million to 205 million bottles. The CIVC also has the power to block part of production in particularly abundant years so that it can continue supplying the market with high-quality products even in poorer years.

The CIVC also provides technical assistance to growers and producers. The vintners of Champagne are determined to continue being world leaders in the technology and know-how applied to the wine that bears their name.

The CIVC has recently approved a quality charter, making product control even stricter. Among the measures included are: compulsory harvesting dates for each class of grapes; selection of clones for each new planting or replanting; and classification of pressing systems.

Moët & Chandon: a brief history

Claude Moët founded the Maison Moët in 1743. He was succeeded by his son, Claude Louis Nicolas (1719–92), and his grandson, Jean-Rémy Moët, who opened new markets in the nineteenth century and brought the firm to its zenith.

In 1832, Jean-Rémy Moët turned the firm over to his son, Victor Moët, and his son-in-law, Pierre-Gabriel Chandon de Briailles, and the name was changed to Moët & Chandon. In 1823 Pierre-Gabriel Chandon had already begun repurchasing the buildings and vineyards that had formerly belonged to the Abbey de Hautvillers, but which had been divided and sold as state property in 1791 during the Revolution. By 1825 the *domaine* was once again complete.

In 1962 Moët & Chandon shares were quoted on the Paris Stock Exchange for the first time. The growth that followed was spectacular.

One out of every four bottles of champagne consumed outside of France is a bottle of Moët & Chandon.

Every second a Moët & Chandon champagne cork pops somewhere in the world.

From the moment it was first created in 1743, Moët & Chandon has been the champagne preferred by some of the world's great personalities, among them Napoleon Bonaparte and Alexander the Great, Tsar of All the Russias. It has been the toast on innumerable historic occasions, was drunk at the coronations of Edward VII, King of Great Britain and Ireland and Emperor of the Indies in 1902, and Queen Elizabeth of England in 1953.

Purveyor to the royal houses of Great Britain, Denmark and Belgium, Moët & Chandon's champagne was served to commemorate such historic events as the bicentennial of the United States of America in 1976 and the 25th Anniversary of Queen Elizabeth's coronation in 1978. Moët & Chandon has flowed at many royal weddings, among them: the wedding of Baudouin I, King of Belgium, in 1960; the wedding of His Serene Highness, Prince Rainier III of Monaco, in 1956; and the wedding of Crown Princess Margrethe of Denmark (now Queen of Denmark) in 1967.

In 1976, Moët & Chandon was served aboard the maiden flight of Concorde. It is the champagne of champions, waiting at the finishing line of the world's great sports events: the world championship Formula 1 automobile races, motorcycle races, motor rallies, the 24-hour Le Mans, the America's Cup sailing race in 1987 and the annual Figaro y La Nioulargue one-man sailing race at St Tropez. Moët & Chandon also has its own equestrian team which competes around the world.

Production

Moët & Chandon produces its world-renowned champagne in Epernay, using grapes purchased largely from local growers and some grapes from its own vines.

Up to the point of *remuage*, or movement of the bottles in order to collect the sediment produced by the secondary fermentation, the production of Moët & Chandon champagne follows the traditional process outlined earlier. Thereafter, the operations of removing the sediment, recorking, wiring, labelling and crating are industrial in scale and almost fully automated. The wine is stored in a warehouse from which orders are prepared for shipment. Shipments of Moët & Chandon in France are prepared in a fully automated warehouse.

Moët & Chandon produces and stores its wines in facilities which occupy an area of 28 square kilometres. Over 160,000 people visit the winery each year.

Control and research

Because Moët & Chandon aims to produce only the highest-quality wines, over twenty different control operations are carried out during the production process. For example, prior to picking, the grapes are assessed in order to determine their maturity and sugar and acid content. Laboratory analyses are carried out several times during the fermentation process (density control, temperature, chromotographic analyses, observation under microscope). Once the fermentation process is complete, the wine is tasted vat by vat in order to decide on the blends.

In the final phase of production, the *vins de reserve* (older wines used for the *coupage*) are carefully checked, as are the *liqueur d'expédition*, the cleanliness of the corks, etc.

Moët & Chandon invests heavily in research, largely dedicated to:

- studying *in vitro* growing techniques (multiplication, grafts, selection);
- improving fermentation;
- studying ageing processes;
- use of the yeast added for the secondary fermentation in bottles in order to facilitate *remuage*.

Moët & Chandon is linked by research contracts to a number of other organizations, among them the University of Reims, BSN (Besnier

Souchon Neuvesel) and Saint-Gobain, that are engaged in projects as varied as studying the composition of wine, how to alter the composition of the bottle glass so that the sediment will slide more easily into the neck, the taste of corks, and isinglass.

Performance and objectives

In 1987 Moët Hennessy SA and Louis Vuitton (owner of Veuve Clicquot, Canard Duchêne and Hueriot champagnes) formed the LVMH Group. The Moët Hennessy SA holding had previously acquired Ruinart (France's oldest champagne producer, founded in 1729) and Mercier (second only to Moët & Chandon).

Exhibits 1–10 and the accompanying text provide further details of Moët & Chandon's performance and current situation. (All information has been provided by the company.)

Moët & Chandon, leader in both the French and export markets, is far and away the most important member of the champagne industry. Its sales are more than double those of its closest competitor.

Moët & Chandon is number one in seven of the ten markets listed above: seven markets which alone account for close to 75% of total champagne exports. Moët & Chandon is second in Canada, third in Switzerland and fourth in the Netherlands. Particularly worth mentioning is the increase in Moët & Chandon's total exports to Spain. These have doubled since 1986 and the firm's market share (46.1%) has increased by more than six points.

Moët & Chandon exports account for 26% of total champagne exports while exports of its closest competitor account for 9%.

The group's own vineyards supply approximately 20% of the grapes required for production. The rest of the grapes are purchased from other growers and account for around 25% of total available grape production.

Also worthy of note is the fact that the group owns vineyards in 13 of the 17 communes whose grapes are ranked as 100%.

- Côte des Blancs: Avize, Chouilly, Cramant, Le Mesnil.
- Montagne de Reims: Ambonnay, Bouzy, Mailly-Champagne, Puisieulx, Sillery, Verzenay, Verzy.
- Vallée de la Marne: Ay-Champagne, Tours-sur-Marne.

Both Moët & Chandon and the group in general are market leaders, but their performance is not enough for the aggressive marketing team, which wants to increase growth still further. But what direction should this growth take? What should be the company's strategy for long-term growth?

Exhibit 1 *Moët & Chandon and the LVMH Group, 1987*

Subsidiary of Moët Hennessy SA
(LVMH Group, Moët Hennessy, Louis Vuitton)

Capital: Moët Hennessy, Louis Vuitton Group	459,562,000 FF
Capital: Moët & Chandon	174,000,000 FF
LVMH Group: consolidated billings	13,170,000,000 FF
Moët & Chandon billings	1,974,500,000 FF
Total shipments of Moët & Chandon	25,170,000 bottles
Exports of which amount to	19,660,000 bottles
Producing vineyards, Moët & Chandon	459 ha
Personnel in Epernay	1,320

Exhibit 2 *Personnel, 1987*

Producer	Total no. employees	Employed in cellars	Employed in vineyards
Moët & Chandon	1,320	423	223
Mercier	241	78	85
Ruinart	67	21	–
Total	1,628	522	308

For the 1987 vintage: Moët & Chandon hired 1,682 pickers, Mercier hired 635 pickers – total: 2,317.

Exhibit 3 *Total champagne exports, 1987 (in bottles)*

	Growers	Shippers	Total
France	64,097,000	72,252,000	136,349,000
Export	5,951,000	75,498,000	81,449,000
Total	70,048,000	147,750,000	217,798,000

Exhibit 4 *Shipments of champagne producers belonging to the Moët Hennessy Group (in bottles) and market share in relation to entire industry, 1987*

Producer	France	Market share (% industry)	Export	Market share (% industry)	Total	Market share (% industry)
Moët & Chandon	5,510,000	7.6	9,660,000	26.0	15,170,000	17.0
Mercier	3,773,000	5.2	837,000	1.1	4,610,000	3.1
Ruinart	981,000	1.4	268,000	0.4	1,249,000	0.9
Total	10,264,000	14.2	10,765,000	27.4	21,029,000	21.0

Exhibit 5 *The champagne group's principal export markets, 1987*

Market	Exports (in bottles)			Market share (%)	
	Total	Group	Moët & Chandon	Group	Moët & Chandon
Great Britain	19,248,000	4,621,000	3,998,000	24.0	20.8
USA	15,837,000	6,881,000	6,884,000	43.0	43.2
West Germany	10,547,000	2,018,000	1,829,000	19.1	17.3
Switzerland	7,264,000	745,000	678,000	10.3	9.3
Italy	7,121,000	2,131,000	2,075,000	29.9	29.1
Belgium	5,243,000	672,000	629,000	12.8	12.0
Netherlands	1,484,000	118,000	109,000	7.9	7.3
Australia	1,007,000	466,000	466,000	46.3	46.3
Canada	1,082,000	217,000	217,000	20.1	20.1
Spain	776,000	368,000	358,000	47.4	46.1

Exhibit 6 *Ranking by continent, 1987*

In 1987 the Moët & Chandon, Mercier and Ruinart Group was:
No. 1 in Europe (EC)   11,125,000 bottles or 20% of the market
No. 1 in the Americas   7,740,000 bottles or 41.5% of the market
No. 1 in Australasia   561,000 bottles or 42.1% of the market
No. 1 in Africa   518,000 bottles or 30.3% of the market
No. 1 in Asia   508,000 bottles or 25.1% of the market

Moët & Chandon is:
No. 1 in Europe   10,179,000 bottles or 18.4% of the market
No. 1 in the Americas   7,700,000 bottles or 41.3% of the market
No. 1 in Australasia   561,000 bottles or 42.1% of the market
No. 1 in Asia   505,000 bottles or 24.9% of the market
No. 1 in Africa   500,000 bottles or 29.3% of the market

Mercier's leading markets are:
Great Britain
West Germany
Italy
Switzerland
Belgium

Ruinart's leading markets are:
West Germany
Switzerland
United States
Italy
Great Britain
Belgium
Sweden
Spain

Exhibit 7   *Share of total export markets, and competitors, 1987*

Moët & Chandon's share of total export markets, 1987 (dealers plus shippers)

Moët & Chandon	24.1%
Closest competitor	8.3%

Market	Moët & Chandon (%)	Closest competitor (%)
Europe	18.4	8.8
Italy	29.1	17.9
Great Britain	20.8	8.6
The Americas (incl. USA)	41.3	15.7
USA	43.2	15.4
Africa	29.3	21.3
Asia–Australasia	31.8	12.4

Exhibit 8   *Vineyards, 1987 harvest*

Vineyards in the Champagne district

Appellation area	34,000 ha (83,980 acres)
Planted area	28,000 ha (69,160 acres)
Producing area	25,566 ha (63,148 acres)

Vineyards belonging to Moët & Chandon and Mercier

Appellation area	866 ha (2,139 acres)
Planted area	702 ha (1,733 acres)
Producing area:	
Moët & Chandon	469 ha (1,158 acres)
Mercier	177 ha (437 acres)

Exhibit 9   *1987 vintage*

	Production volume for entire Champagne district	
	1987	1986
In *pièces* (205 litres)	967,334	953,982
In hectolitres	1,983,000	1,956,000
Equivalent in bottles (after losses)	260,434,000	256,888,000

Grape prices
21.77 francs per kg for grapes classified as 100%
Price in 1986: 22.19 francs/kg

Exhibit 10   *Stock at 1 January 1988*

The equivalent stock in bottles for the champagne group (bottles in wine cellars, *vins de reserve*, wine in vats) amounted to *106 million bottles* on 1 January 1988. The breakdown was as follows:

Moët & Chandon	87 million bottles
Mercier	14 million bottles
Ruinart	5 million bottles

Exhibit 11　*Extent of wine cellars*

Moët & Chandon	28 kilometres (17.5 miles)
Mercier	18 kilometres (11 miles)
Ruinart	8 kilometres (5 miles)

Exhibit 12　*Number of visitors to cellars, 1987*

Producer	French	Other nationalities	Total
Moët & Chandon	56,303	89,940	146,243
Mercier	99,687	37,976	137,663
Ruinart	8,379	4,065	12,444
Total	164,369	131,981	296,350

Questions for discussion/suggested tasks

In the light of the above, participants should consider the strategies available to Moët & Chandon to achieve their growth objectives. In doing so, you should also address the following:

1　What are the key environmental and other factors affecting the potential growth and development of Moët & Chandon?
2　What are the threats and opportunities facing the company?
3　What are the most important aspects of the market, competition, product and related consumer behaviour?

Appendix 1: Dom Pérignon (1639–1715)

Dom Pérignon is the famous Benedictine monk known to history for discovering the secret of Champagne wines during the reign of Louis XIV, the Sun King. Born in 1639 in Sainte-Menehould, in Champagne, he entered the Abbey of Saint-Vannes-de-Verdun as a novice and was then transferred to Hautvillers, where he spent the remaining forty-seven years of his life as the abbey's cellarer.

A skilled taster and blender of wines and a tireless worker, he managed to make the grey and red still wines of Champagne into the renowned sparkling beverage known to the royal court as Father Pérignon's wine, the Devil's wine and the cork blaster.

Dom Pérignon's success lies in his discovery of five principal elements that comprise the secret of Champagne wine:

- blending grapes and wine from different vineyards in order to produce the *cuvée* or wine from a single vintage;

- rapid pressing, with the black grapes thinly spread over a large surface in order to ensure that the must is a clear as glass;
- use of the first thick, resistant glass bottles, which in Dom Pérignon's day were pear-shaped;
- using a Spanish cork stopper instead of the traditional hemp-covered wooden cylinder and tying it down with cord to keep the foam from escaping;
- digging caves in chalky soil to guarantee that the wines are aged at a constant temperature and simultaneously to limit bursts.

In addition to these important discoveries, great progress was made in growing and selecting the grapes, and caring for the vineyards of Champagne.

Now owned by Moët & Chandon, the museum of the Abbey of Hautvillers provides a glimpse of the daily life of the monks in the seventeenth century and recounts the rich history of the abbey.

Appendix 2: The viticulture of Champagne

The grape-producing area is strictly defined under the terms of the law of 22 July 1927. It accounts for about 2% of France's total wine-growing area. Each municipality carefully catalogues the vineyards whose grapes are destined for the production of champagne wine.

The vineyards of Champagne are not all ranked equally. They are catalogued in several zones which vary in importance. Most of the vineyards are located in the Department of the Marne.

La Montagne de Reims is a spacious plateau that slopes gently down to meet the valleys of the Vesle and Arde in the north and the Marne in the south. The vines grow thickly along the sides of the plateau. Among the best *crus* are those which come from the valleys of Ambonnay, Beaumont-sur-Vesle, Bouzy, Louvois, Mailly-Champagne, Sillery, Verzenay and Verzy.

The Marne Valley covers about 100 square kilometres, stretching from Sâacy-sur-Marne in the Department of Seine-et-Marne to Tours-sur-Marne beyond Epernay. Quite sparse in the Department of Aisne, the vines grow more thickly starting at Château-Thierry, and from Darmans the vineyards stretch out as far as the eye can see, covering the rolling hills which slope more or less gently down to the banks of the river, and thriving too in the curious, wavy depressions of land which border the valley. The most famous vineyards are those of Ay and Mareuil-sur-Ay.

La Côte des Blancs almost exclusively produces white grapes, hence its name. It is a steep cliff, perpendicular to the Montagne de Reims, located south of Epernay. The vines of Avize, Cramant, Oger and Mesnil-sur-Oger are the most renowned.

South of the Department of the Marne the vines grow sparsely around Sezanne, a small but charming town.

In the Vitry-le-François region, cultivation is restricted to a few municipalities and production is extremely limited.

The vines of the Department of the Aube stretch southward and are largely grouped around the towns of Bar-sur-Seine and Bar-sur-Aube, with the exception of the area around Villenauxe-la Grande, whose vineyards are actually an extension of those in southern Marne, and Montgueux, in the immediate vicinity of Troyes, where only a dozen hectares of vineyards are located.

The Department of the Haute-Marne is located to the east of Bar-sur-Aube, just after Colombey-les-deux-Eglises, and a few hectares of vineyards are located there.

At the beginning of the century, phylloxera destroyed all the original vines, only part of which were replanted. At the end of the second World War only 11,000 hectares were producing grapes. In 1956 replanting began in earnest and now 25,000 hectares are devoted to growing grapes for champagne wine.

The growing area is broken down as follows:

18,000 ha in the Department of the Marne (75%)
4,200 ha in the Department of the Aube (17%)
2,000 ha in the Department of l'Aisne and Seine-et-Marne (8%).

The growing area, with its particular chalky subsoil, is officially defined by French law and covers an area of 34,000 hectares, roughly 25,000 hectares of which are under cultivation. It embraces 250 different villages or vineyards (*crus*), each one with its own particular characteristics. Champagne may not be produced outside the limits of this region.

Only three types of grapes may be used to produce champagne: Pinot Noir, a generous, powerful grape; Chardonnay, a strong white grape with a good deal of finesse; and Pinot Meunier, a light, delicate grape.

Appendix 3: How to read a champagne label

The final touch is the label, which is affixed just before the champagne is sent out. The label is like a signature of authentication. Every label must contain the following information:

- the word champagne in large letters;
- the name of the brand or producer;
- the registration number assigned by the CIVC, preceded by the initials which identify the manufacturer;
- the capacity of the bottle.

Other information which might be included consists of details such as:

- the location of the producer or wine merchant;
- the year of preparation if it is a *millésime* wine;
- description of the *cuvée* such as *blanc de blancs* or *rosé*;

- the degree of sweetness, in ascending order: *brut, extra-dry, sec, demi-sec* and *doux*.

Terms used on the label

Blanc de blancs. This means that the champagne is made exclusively from Chardonnay white grapes.

Blanc de noirs. This means just the opposite: the champagne is made exclusively from black Pinot Noir grapes (the colour is in the grape skin and unless the must comes into contact with the skin it is naturally white).

Crémant. This champagne has much less pressure than other varieties (2.5–3 atmospheres rather than 4–5). The foam is creamy and disappears quickly. *Crémant* wines have more bouquet and the characteristics of the different varieties are more pronounced.

Cru is wine from a single vineyard. Use of the expression *grand cru* signifies that the vineyard belongs to a commune or municipality whose grapes are considered the best and ranked as 100% on the price scale. *Premier cru* is ranked between 90% and 100% on the price scale.

Grand cru. Vineyards or *crus* located in the Champagne district are classified according to a complicated system linked to the price of grapes. Prices are set each year using the best (or 100%) vineyards as the point of reference on a scale that descends to 70%. The percentage indicates the price to be paid in relation to the 100% price. The Mailly growers' co-operative is able to specialize in 100% champagnes because all the vineyards in Mailly commune have this top ranking.

Millésme. This means that the champagne has been produced with wine from a single particularly good vintage. These champagnes are always better than the average (and particularly cherished by their producers) wines which are a blend of several *coupages*.

Premier cru is also wine from a single vineyard, but with the difference that the municipality where it is located is ranked between 90% and 100% on the scale of grape prices. These wines always have a good deal of personality even though they are not as balanced as the *grands crus*.

Réserve. A meaningless adjective which can be used by any champagne.

Sweetness: Brut is a wine to which no *liqueur d'expédition* (the sweet mixture added after *dégorgement*) or less than 0.5% has been added. *Extra-sec*: the *liqueur d'expédition* amounts to 1–2%. *Demi-sec*: 6–8% liqueur. *Doux*: up to 14% *liqueur d'expédition*.

CM. The brand is the property of a growers' co-operative association.

MA means that the name of the wine is an authorized brand (normally wine produced by the growers themselves or a vintner and sold by another).

NM. When the registration number is preceded by these two letters it means that the product bears the actual name of the company which purchases the wine from the growers and produces the champagne.

RM. The wine bears the name of the *recoltant-manipulant* (grower-handler) who produces and sells the wine from his or her own vineyards.

2

Moët & Chandon B
A diversification of strategy

Guillermo Cisneros and Jordi Montaña

This case is a continuation of 'Moët & Chandon A' and examines the company's attempt to diversify by producing a sparkling wine (*cava*) in the Spanish market. Spain has a long tradition of producing sparkling wines. The issues raised by the case relate to how Moët & Chandon might best go about the development of a *cava* in terms of target markets, product concept and positioning, and international development and marketing.

And Moët & Chandon came to Spain

The world leader in the champagne market decided to invest in Spain. Together with its distributor in Spain, Aferfrans, Moët & Chandon embarked on a joint venture, opening its own wine cellars in the Penedès district. The result? Chandon sparkling wine, or *cava*.

Moët & Chandon is simultaneously faced with a growing world demand for its product and the problem of production restrictions. The Champagne district of France has reached its production limit. That is why Moët & Chandon ventured abroad as early as 1960, producing its wines first in Argentina, where it quickly became the leading producer of sparkling wines, and later in Brazil, California, West Germany and Australia. But the situation is very different in Spain.

First of all, Spain has traditionally produced sparkling wines. Furthermore, the EC-imposed differentiation between *cava* and champagne is abundantly clear. Rather than fighting against this, Moët & Chandon has gone straight to the Penedès, the heart of Spain's sparkling-wine-producing area, and announced that it is going to produce *cava* there, marketing it under the brand name Chandon. Its idea is to compete with the top-quality *cavas* on the Spanish market, keeping production fairly low and setting top-of-the-line prices, i.e. 1,500–1,800 pesetas per bottle.

Cava vs champagne: the bubble war

When Spain joined the EC it was no longer allowed to use the word 'champagne' for the Catalan sparkling wines produced by the *méthode champenoise*. Not content with that, France, supported by Italy and West Germany, requested that the use of the descriptive phrase *méthode champenoise* on the labels likewise be prohibited. In November 1985 the EC Council of Ministers again decided in favour of France. But the conditions were not as strict as the Catalan producers had feared: they were given an eight-year transition period, during which they may continue to use the description on bottles destined for other EC countries. For exports to non-EC countries they may continue to use the words *méthode champenoise* indefinitely.

This decision met with every conceivable sort of reaction, from absolute outrage to opinions that the restrictions might eventually work in Spain's favour. One definite result is that the publicity about the whole issue and the subsequent institutional advertising campaign managed to make *cava* almost a household word. Furthermore, interest from abroad has not declined. Paradoxically, while vintners from Champagne have managed to protect their cherished *appellation d'origine* the same cannot be said for their counterparts in the Penedès: Spanish law permits sparkling wine from any region in Spain to be labelled *cava*.

Some questions still remain to be answered. Are *cava* and champagne really the same product but with different names? Just how important are these differences in provenance? We will try to answer these questions on the following pages.

Differences and similarities between *cava* and champagne

The characteristics of cava

The grapes used in *cava* are grown in sandy soil with a chalky underlay in a climate with average annual temperatures of 15°C and highs of more than 30°C during the summer months, an average of 2,500 hours of sunshine per year and 500 mm of rain annually.

The most-used varieties of grape are Xarelo, Macebeo, Parellada and Monastrell. Picking starts at the end of August. Once picked, the grapes are quickly transported to the vintners, where they are pressed to obtain a maximum of 84 hectolitres for every hectare of vines.

Cava is produced according to the *méthode champenoise*, starting with grapes whose alcoholic content is 10% and which undergo a secondary fermentation lasting at least nine months. The wine is aged in the bottle for an average of two or more years.

A peculiarity of the production process is that the temperatures of fermentation must be corrected due to the extreme heat at the time of picking. This gives a pale sparkling wine with a yellowy-green tinge. Its flavour is not particularly sour, but dry and fruity. The aroma depends on the type of grape used. There is also a slightly yeasty fragrance. Because *cava* is younger than champagne it tends to be more effervescent, with larger bubbles.

Vintages are so regular that *millémisation* or mention of the particular vintage is not necessary.

Champagne

Champagne is produced from Pinot and Pinot Noir black grapes and from Chardonnay whites, grown in chalky ground containing silex. The climate in the Champagne district is not as predictable as in the Penedès, and thus vintages are very irregular. Average temperatures are 10°C with 1,700 hours of sunshine per year and 500 mm of rain. Picking begins in mid-October, and the grapes are pressed right in the vineyards, obtaining a maximum of 50 hectolitres per hectare. The must is transported to the vintners, where the wine is produced by the *méthode champenoise*.

Unlike *cava*, different wines are blended according to the ranking of the vineyard to form *cuvée*. If the wine is exceptional, it is not blended with any other, and this, together with the year of the vintage, is mentioned on the label.

The wine has a strength of 8–9° at the outset of secondary fermentation. This is boosted to 10° during fermentation, which lasts at least twelve months. The wine is generally aged in the bottle for three to eight years. The final product is a yellow sparkling wine with greenish highlights, delicate bubbles, an intensely floral perfume and a spicy, floral flavour, mellower yet more acid than its Spanish counterpart. Because the grapes are more sour, the French cannot produce a *brut nature*, and some sugar must always be added to champagne during secondary fermentation.

Producing sparkling wines

There are three ways to produce sparkling wines: the *méthode champenoise*, or Dom Pérignon's method, used in producing champagne and *cava*; the transfer method; and the *grand vase* or tank method.

Méthode champenoise According to official regulations, the *méthode champenoise* means the production of a natural sparkling wine in which the entire process, from secondary fermentation to elimination of the lees, or sediment, takes place in the same bottle in which *tirage* took place. The process involves the following steps:

1 *Tirage*: yeast and sugar are added to the base wine before bottling, in order to produce secondary fermentation.
2 Corking: the bottles are hermetically sealed.
3 Ageing in the cellar: the bottles are left on their sides until all the sugar has been converted to alcohol or gas.
4 *Remuage*: the bottles are now stacked neck downwards in wooden racks called *pupitres*, in order to work down the sediment in the bottle till it nearly covers the cork. The bottles are given a twist every day until they reach a perpendicular position.
5 *Dégorgement*: extraction of the sediment-covered cork by means of freezing the wine in the neck of the bottle to a solid lump of ice.
6 Final corking and labelling: the base of the final cork will be stamped with a four-pointed star to show that the sparkling wine was produced according to the *méthode champenoise*.

The transfer method Natural sparkling wines may also be produced by the transfer method, in which the wine ferments in the same bottle used for the *tirage* and is later decanted to another in order to eliminate the sediment. Fermentation lasts a minimum of two years. The steps involved in producing wine by the transfer method are:

1 *Tirage*: yeast and sugar are added to the base wine before bottling, in order to produce secondary fermentation.
2 Filtering and decanting: after at least two months in a horizontal position, the sparkling wine is filtered, in order to eliminate the sediment, and then decanted to another bottle. A large rectangle is stamped on the bottom of the cork to indicate that the wine was produced by this method.

The méthode grand vase *or tank method* When sparkling wine is produced by the *méthode grand vase*, secondary fermentation takes place in hermetically sealed vats. After a minimum of twenty-one days has passed, the wine is filtered and bottled. A circle 7 mm in diameter is stamped on the bottom of the cork to indicate that the wine was produced by the *méthode grand vase*.

More details about cava and champagne

Sugar content Wines to which no sugar has been added are called *brut nature*. When sugar has been added the wines are classified in ascending order of sweetness as *brut*, *extra-dry*, *dry* and *semi-dry*.

Millésime In a particularly good year, the *cuvée*, or blend of musts, can be made exclusively with wines from that particular vintage to produce *champagne millésime*. This is the only champagne whose labels mention the vintage.

Bottle sizes Champagne and *cava* are available in the following sized bottles:

- quarter-bottle (or split): 20 cl;
- half-bottle: 37.5 cl (2 glasses);
- bottle: 75 cl (6 glasses);
- magnum: 150 cl (2 bottles);
- jeroboam: 4 bottles;
- rehoboam: 6 bottles;
- methuselah: 8 bottles;
- salmanazar: 12 bottles;
- balthazar: 16 bottles
- nebuchadnezzar: 20 bottles.

The cava and champagne markets in Spain (notably Catalonia)

The Spanish sparkling wine market

Spain produces 123 million bottles of sparkling wine per year. Ninety-seven per cent of them are *cavas* produced according to the *méthode champenoise*. Seventy-five per cent of production, or about 90 million bottles, remain in Spain. The other 25% are exported. Ninety-nine per cent of sparkling wine production takes place in Catalonia, and 75% of that comes from the town of San Sadurní de Anoia.

Figures from the MAPA panel reveal that sparkling wines account for 0.3% of food and drink purchases in Spain. Average consumption per person per year amounts to 1.3 litres. In metropolitan areas sparkling wines account for a larger part of the family budget than in more rural areas. (All information has been provided by Moët & Chandon.)

Catalonia is also the region that consumes the most *cava*. Catalonia and Aragon together account for 55% of Spanish consumption. Nielsen statistics give the following breakdown of Spanish regions according to

Exhibit 1 *Consumption of Spanish wines in Spain (annual average)*

	National	Metropolitan areas
Amount purchased (litres/inhab./year)	1.3	1.5
% of purchaser houtholds	8.2	9.7
Amount spent (ptas/inhab./year)	440	552
Price (ptas/litre)	345.6	366.6

Source: MAPA panel figures, published by ARAL, 1986

Exhibit 2   *Regional share of sparkling wine consumption, 1986 (%)*

Greater Barcelona Area	31
Catalonia/Aragon	24
Levante	11
Andalusia	6
Northern-central Spain	13
Madrid	9
Other	6
Total	100

Source: A.C. Nielsen

their consumption of sparkling wines shown in Exhibit 2 (figures are for 1986, but there have been no major changes since then).

The MAPA panel figures (1986) also show that Catalonia and the Greater Barcelona Area are the largest consumers of sparkling wines. Thus the average number of households purchasing *cava* per year is 14.7% of total households in north-east Spain as opposed to a national average of 8.2%. Average annual consumption in the north-east is 2.4 litres per inhabitant, and the amount spent annually on *cava* is 876 pesetas per person, almost twice the national average. In addition, consumers in this region pay the highest prices per litre (411.5 pesetas).

The city of Barcelona is outstanding among the country's metropolitan areas. MAPA figures for Barcelona are 2.4 litres per inhabitant and 974 pesetas spent annually per inhabitant on *cava* at an average price of 401 pesetas per litre.

The MAPA panel, like the Nielsen survey, indicates that Andalusia and the Canary Islands are the parts of Spain that consume the least sparkling wine. Annual average consumption per inhabitant amounts to 0.6 litres in Andalusia and 0.4 litres in the Canary Islands.

Sparkling wines are an extremely seasonal drink. While the average monthly consumption of sparkling wines in Spain is 0.7 litres, consumption increases to 4.0 litres in December. Fifty per cent of spending on sparkling wine takes place in December when the purchase of *cava* accounts for 1.8% of household food budgets. In other words, not only do people drink more *cava* during the holiday season, they also spend more money on it.

Although there are no specific figures, available indications are that *cava* is gradually becoming a less seasonal drink, particularly in the Greater Barcelona Area and the rest of Catalonia. People drink *cava* at home. According to the MAPA, approximately 80.4% of the sparkling wine drunk in Spain is drunk in the home, while 19.6% is drunk in restaurants, bars, nightclubs and other public places.

Self-service markets account for the largest volume of sales: 50–55%. Specialized wine merchants sell 30–33% of all sparkling wines.

Exports

One of the most important features of the Spanish sparkling wine industry is the increase in exports. This amounted to a real boom between 1981 and 1984 but then tapered off slightly. Export figures for Spanish sparkling wines for 1980–6 are shown in Exhibit 3.

Exhibit 3 *Exports of Spanish sparkling wines, 1980–6*

	No. bottles	Annual growth rate (%)	Sales (000 ptas)	Annual growth in sales (%)
1980	10,048,000	–	1,097,975	–
1981	13,896,000	38.3	1,845,737	68.5
1982	17,952,580	29.2	2,961,232	60.5
1983	23,049,921	28.4	4,650,334	46.9
1984	27,447,060	19.1	6,184,208	32.9
1985	30,769,357	12.1	7,089,537	14.6
1986	32,089,550	4.3	7,127,956	0.5

In 1986 *cava* accounted for 96.7% of all Spanish sparkling wine exports; 31,044,176 bottles of *cava* were exported. The United States is Spain's largest customer for sparkling wines, accounting for 60% of exports. This goes a long way towards explaining the difference in export growth per unit and per price in pesetas. As can be seen in Exhibit 3, the amount of exports in pesetas at first showed a greater increase than exports by number of bottles. By 1986 the situation was just the opposite, and the increase was greater in the number of bottles exported than in the volume of sales in pesetas. This is explained by fluctuations in the value of the dollar.

In 1986 the leading purchasers of Spanish sparkling wines were as shown in Exhibit 4.

Exhibit 4 *Export purchasers of Spanish sparkling wines, 1986*

	No. bottles
USA	18,516,251
Canada	13,596,688
Germany	2,161,253
Great Britain	1,224,548
Sweden	1,000,711
Italy	500,501
Japan	391,187
Venezuela	368,400
Denmark	366,952
Netherlands	329,580

Imports

Since Spain became a member of the EC there has been a notable increase in imports of sparkling wine, particularly champagne. In 1986, 97.6% of the litres imported came from France, which also accounted for 99.5% of the cost of sparkling wine imports. The provenance and volume of 1985 and 1986 imports are shown in Exhibit 5.

Exhibit 5   *Spanish imports of sparkling wine, 1985 and 1986*

Source country	1985		1986	
	Litres	000 ptas	Litres	000 ptas
France	163,995	201,822	387,590	647,160
Italy	101	281	132	552
Netherlands	2	2	–	–
West Germany	–	–	9,244	2,008

Source: ARAL, based on figures from the Spanish Customs Authority

Growth in sparkling wine imports (141% in litres and 295% in pesetas between 1985 and 1986) continued at the same pace in 1987. When imports during the first half of 1986 are compared with those of the same period a year earlier, we can see that total sparkling wine imports registered an increase of 110% in litres and 221% in pesetas. In these same periods, imports from France increased 51.1% in litres and 96.2% in pesetas. These figures were also provided by ARAL and based on figures from the Spanish Customs Authority.

Two important trends can be noted. First, the number of litres of sparkling wine imported from France is on the decline. However, in financial terms France's market share is by far the highest of any country – see Exhibit 6.

Exhibit 6   *French share of sparkling wine imports, 1985–7*

	Litres (%)	Pesetas (%)
1985	99.8	99.9
1986	97.6	99.5
1st half of 1987	71.8	95.8

Secondly, imports are increasing more in qualitative terms than in quantitative ones. In other words, imports can be said to be increasingly expensive. As is clearly shown in Exhibit 5, the increases are far greater in financial terms than in the number of litres imported. Imports of champagne would appear to be largely responsible for the increased cost of imports. The fact that France's market share remains steady in financial terms while registering a decrease in the number of litres imported would seem to bear out this hypothesis.

Champagne imports

According to figures from the Comité Interprofessionnel du Vin de Champagne, Spain imported 445,699 bottles of champagne in 1986, up 118.51% from a year earlier. This upward tendency continued during the first half of 1987, when imports registered an 81.8% increase, making Spain the world's ninth largest importer of champagne.

The brand leader is Moët & Chandon, with imports of 179,770 bottles in 1986. In 1985 and 1986 the leading brands were as shown in Exhibit 7.

Exhibit 7 *Leading brands of champagne imported into Spain, 1985 and 1986*

1985[1]		1986[2]	
Brand	No. bottles	Brand	No. bottles
Moët & Chandon	107,194	Moët & Chandon	179,770
Veuve Clicquot	32,832	Henri Abelé	58,922
Mumm	27,766	Mumm	56,042
Laurent Perrier	22,119	Veuve Clicquot	47,320
Krug	3,810	Laurent Perrier	24,126
Louis Roederer	3,236	Louis Roederer	17,942
Charles Heidsieck	2,500	Pommery	12,024
Besserat de Bellefon	2,498	Krug	9,210
Taittinger	2,028	Ruinart	7,200
Piper Heidsieck	1,813	Pol Roger	4,360
Bollinger	1,704		

[1] Total champagne imports in 1985 – 216,849 bottles.
[2] Total champagne imports in 1986 – 455,699 bottles.

Champagne accounts for the bulk of sparkling wine imported from France. Although there is some disparity in the figures given by different sources, it would appear that champagne's share of total French sparkling wine imports has registered a slight decline. Assuming that each bottle contains an average of 0.75 litres, champagne accounted for 99% of all French sparkling wine imports into Spain in 1985, while in 1986 this figure dropped to 88%.

While still the leading importer, Moët & Chandon's market share has declined slightly, and sales increases were proportionately lower for Moët & Chandon than for champagne as a whole. Moët & Chandon accounted for 49.4% of all champagne imports in 1985 and for 39.4% in 1986.

Special mention must be made of Henri Abelé, which was the second-ranking champagne in 1986, with 12.9% of all imports. This was almost certainly due to the fact that Henri Abelé was purchased by Freixenet, a Catalan producer of *cava*.

The competition

Freixenet and Codorníu are Spain's two leading brands of sparkling wines produced by the *méthode champenoise*. The two companies account for the lion's share of both the Spanish and export markets. The strategies of the two companies are markedly different and warrant special attention. Ranking just behind the two leaders are a number of medium-sized producers such as Juvé Camps, Marqués de Monistrol and Masachs, with annual sales of about 1,000 million pesetas.

One of the most noteworthy trends in the industry is the growth in the number of small producers with much lower sales figures, who are taking advantage of the boom in *cava*. While there were 65 producers of *cava* registered in 1977, the number had almost tripled, to 173, by 1987.

Freixenet

Freixenet is the largest producer of Spanish *cava*, with 1987 sales of over 20,000 million pesetas. The Freixenet brands are Carta Nevada, Cordón Negro, Gloria Ferrer (produced in California), Segura Viudas, Castellblanch, Conde de Caralt, Canals Nubiola and Dubois. In addition, Freixenet owns the French champagne producer Henri Abelé.

Freixenet is known for its aggressive marketing techniques, broad product range, volume of production and a focus on export markets. Its acceptance on the US market is a real phenomenon. Thanks to its sales network and an advertising campaign that urges the public to celebrate those 'small, everyday victories', Freixenet has become Spain's largest exporter of sparkling wine to the United States, outperforming even brands like Moët & Chandon. Freixenet has also invested heavily abroad, most notably in California's Sonoma Valley near San Francisco, where the Gloria Ferrer brand is produced for the US market, and in France, where Freixenet purchased Henri Abelé, one of the country's most reputable producers of champagne. As a result of this purchase, Henri Abelé soared to second place among champagne exporters to Spain in 1987.

Codorníu

The Codorníu brands are Codorníu, Delapierre, Rondel and Raimat. Although Codorníu ranks second in terms of sales (16,000 million pesetas in 1987) it is the leading brand in Spain. While Freixenet places its faith in exports, Codorníu aims largely at the domestic market or exports to other EC countries. The company prefers to give priority to its up-market products rather than stressing volume and a mass market. Although Codorníu has made a few direct investments abroad, particularly in vineyards in California, purchased some years ago but not yet in operation, the company has preferred to enter foreign markets through distribution agreements with other firms (Marie Brizard in France, Fernet Branca in Italy).

Other cavas *from the Penedès*

As mentioned earlier, Marqués de Monistrol (owned by Martini), Juvé Camps and Masachs are outstanding among the remaining producers of *cava*. Juvé Camps is a family business which aims to produce high-quality *cava* and to grow slowly but steadily (about 5% per year). The company hopes eventually to become self-sufficient in grape production so that it can better control the quality of its wines. Its Reserva de la Familia is produced in limited amounts, and demand always exceeds the supply, which invariably sells out in record time. Masach markets Louis de Vernier, Carolina de Masachs and Masachs, working with an independent distributor which has contributed greatly to the company's success.

Other producers whose sales have spiralled in the past few years are Parxet, Vallformosa, Torelló, Ferret, Mont-Rubí, Rovellats, Nadal, Mont-Marçal and Gramona, whose products are generally preferred by expert wine tasters and contest judges. Most of the smaller producers are family businesses and produce *cava* according to traditional, non-automated methods, carefully selecting their grapes and ageing the wine according to their own particular criteria.

Moët & Chandon: decision to produce *cava* and qualitative research findings

One of the options in Moët & Chandon's growth strategy was to move into the sparkling wine market (see 'Moët & Chandon A'). The company had already done this in California, Brazil and Australia. The Spanish sparkling wine market was attractive, and the company was inclined to take the step. However, there were some doubts about Spanish consumer behaviour, and these had to be closely studied before deciding on the brand policy to use when introducing Moët & Chandon *cava*.

The following are the principal findings of the group meetings which were part of the ESADE research commissioned by Moët & Chandon. This was the first research project carried out under the terms of Moët & Chandon's Observatoire programme whereby management schools in different countries collaborate in the company's marketing research. The study was directed by Guillermo Cisneros, who was assisted by ESADE's

Empresa Joventut association, and Professor Lluís Martinez-Ribes, who directed one of the group meetings.

The objective of these group meetings was to obtain information on:

- the image of *cava* and champagne;
- purchasing and drinking habits;
- images of brands, bottles, labels;
- attitudes towards a Chandon *cava*.

Main findings from the group meetings

Cava vs champagne

The meetings began with a question about the perceived difference between *cava* and champagne. The replies revealed that a considerable difference is perceived between *cava* and champagne. Perception varies according to the respondent's familiarity with the subject. Awareness of a difference was further revealed when participants were asked to rank brands by quality. At the first meeting an actual physical space was left between the bottles of *cava* and the bottles of champagne. When the participants were asked if this space reflected a difference between the two products, they replied that it did. In other words, *cava* and champagne were two very different things.

Champagne is seen as the *French* one, from Champagne. People are not too sure about the exact differences between the two products, but they know that champagne always comes from France and that *it is of better quality*: 'It's got more prestige'; 'It's a whole different story.' Some of the more knowledgeable participants referred to differences in the effervescence, the type of grape and soil. Comments went so far as to state that champagne 'goes down better' and *tastes different*. Only rarely was any mention made of differences in the production processes, which were generally believed to be similar.

Cava is seen as local, from Catalonia. In both group meetings some mention was made of a certain 'chauvinism' or 'patriotism' which led Catalans to opt for their own product, *cava*. The term *cava* has been adopted fairly quickly, and the groups felt that the name was a good choice.

Drinking and purchasing habits

One important difference between *cava* and champagne is the occasion for drinking it:

Cava is an everyday drink, for 'school parties'. When a bottle of *cava* is uncorked you expect to hear a 'pop' and see the cork fly. It's quite common to have a bottle of *cava* in the refrigerator at all times, ready to open at a family dinner, when friends drop around, at the slightest excuse.

Champagne is for special occasions, really important events. The *ritual* is important for both products, but more so for champagne, and is observed from the moment it is purchased until the moment it is drunk. When people buy champagne they buy *good champagne, not just any champagne*. It must be uncorked ceremoniously, with a lot of care.

Furthermore, champagne makes the best *gift*. It makes a good impression. It is a guarantee that you are giving a good present, something special.

As far as purchasing habits are concerned, we find that *the purchaser is invariably the male, particularly in the case of champagne*. Women are not usually connoisseurs. Besides, they have a budget to stick to when they go shopping. Men don't pay much attention to prices. They don't pay any attention to budgets. Furthermore, purchases like this are extras, above and beyond the normal budget. There is a ritual involved even in purchasing champagne, especially when it is being purchased for a special occasion, and it is important to get just the right brand.

There are two ways of purchasing champagne:

- Staying on the 'safe side': you're buying it for an occasion and you want to make a good impression; you buy a well-known brand, one you know won't disappoint you; you stay on sure ground.
- Experimenting: you buy it for yourself, not for anyone else; you look for lesser-known, high-quality brands.

A number of people commented that when you buy something exceptional, like champagne, you usually buy it with someone else.

Recommendations seem to be important, but even more so is the person who introduces you to a particular product (champagne) or a particularly good brand.

It would appear that the older people are, the more quality conscious they become. Brand loyalty also appears to be greater among older people.

As far as *where* champagne is purchased, participants in the study commented that you can find champagne anywhere, even in huge supermarkets. Still, when the time comes to buy something special like champagne, people tend to go to specialty shops where there is not only a good assortment of brands, but also knowledgeable personnel.

Brand images

Among the brands used in the meetings, both groups *dismissed* Henri Abelé, Beaumet, Marcet and Roederer *because they were unknown*.

As mentioned earlier, when the brands were arranged by quality, all the *cavas* were grouped on one side and all the champagnes on the other. The champagnes were all considered to be of better quality.

Among the champagnes there was no clear leader as far as quality was concerned. There were discussions about whether the best was Veuve

Clicquot or Moët & Chandon, which was considered among the best and, according to some people, the very best.

Among the *cavas*, most respondents felt that Codorníu, particularly Gran Codorníu, was the best. Anna de Codorníu was also considered a good *cava*. Some people nominated Juvé Camps' Gran Reserva de la Familia as the best *cava*.

In terms of each brand's subjective identity/meaning to the consumer, the respondents felt that:

- *Moët & Chandon* is champagne *par excellence Moët & Chandon is synonymous with champagne, and champagne is synonymous with Moët & Chandon.* 'When you've got something important to celebrate, you buy a good champagne; you buy Moët & Chandon.' The brand appears to be *rich in symbolism*, with an aura of *tradition and prestige*. Moët & Chandon is a guarantee. When you buy Moët & Chandon you know *you won't make a mistake*; you're buying a certain quality and won't be disappointed.
- *Veuve Clicquot* and *Mumm* are simply considered good brands of champagne, without the symbolism of Moët & Chandon. They are brands for sybarites, people who are more expert on the subject of champagnes.
- Like its champagne counterpart, Moët & Chandon, *Codorníu* is the *cava par excellence*. It has *distinction, tradition*. With Codorníu you know you're on safe ground; there's no danger of making a mistake. It's a brand that consistently gives good quality, and, above all, the quality/price ratio is good. We could say that *Codorníu is the Moët & Chandon of* cavas.
- *Freixenet* is *mass-produced*, commercial.
- *Juvé Camps* is a good brand of *cava*; according to some people, the very best. Others felt that its sales success has caused it to become more of a mass product and this has had a considerable effect on its quality.

Participants in the study particularly noted the absence of certain smaller, but high-quality, *cavas*.

Bottles and labels

Different-shaped bottles in different colours and with various styles of labels were used in order to compare preferences, particularly in relation to the Moët & Chandon bottle.

About bottles The traditional-shaped bottle is the best liked. Odd-shaped, extravagant bottles are almost unanimously regarded with suspicion. The 'typical' bottle, e.g. the Moët Brut Imperial bottle, is the preferred shape and gives the prospective customer the greatest feeling of confidence in the content of the bottle.

Very pale or transparent bottles are clearly rejected. However, completely opaque bottles, like Freixenet's Cordón Negro, are also rejected. Dark green is considered the right colour for the bottle.

The cork: two basic designs were presented – the traditional foil-covered cork and the cork held fast with wire clamps. The wire clamp was flatly rejected. At first it was used by certain brands to indicate that the wine was not produced by industrial methods, but it quickly became fashionable with any small manufacturer who wanted to foist off a quite ordinary *cava* as something special. As a result, the clamp fastening has lost its charm, and people even have a certain aversion to it. The traditional cork with its foil hood is definitely the preferred. Should the clamp system be used, consumers prefer the cork to be covered in foil.

Labels This may well be the most important contribution to brand image. Participants in the study observed that champagne labels were in the same style as wine labels, and differed considerably from *cava* labels.

Consumers prefer both champagne and *cava* labels to be conservative. As a result the preferred *cava* labels were Juvé Camps (which some people considered the best looking, the most serious, the ideal) and Codorníu (Anna de Codorníu). In fact, the Anna de Codorníu label was considered the most 'champagne-like'. People did not like the Brut Barroco or Laixertelle labels.

The least-liked champagne label was Mumm's, which reminded people of Paternina Banda Roja wine labels. The Henri Abelé label was also widely disliked because of the colour combination used.

Moët & Chandon (Brut Imperial) was among the preferred labels. When the labels for Moët & Chandon Brut Imperial and Brut Imperial 82 were compared, the lighter-coloured label was preferred in some, but not all, cases. Those who liked it again cited its 'seriousness', the fact that it was a typical label. Still, the green label was not without its good points. In some cases it was considered to have a better 'finish' (this observation also referred to the collar label, and the foil capsule or covering of the cork).

Both groups unanimously agreed that the ribbon and red seal on the Moët & Chandon bottle were superfluous and clashed with the rest of the bottle. Opinions about the foil-covered cork were favourable. The rough texture of the foil used for Brut Imperial 82 was particularly well liked. Furthermore, this covering or capsule is considered an important part of the bottle and it should be selected with care (for example, the texture or lack of same on the Juvé Camps foil coverings was felt to detract from the rest of the bottle).

A good deal of importance was given to brand symbolism when ranking labels. The brand itself was considered more important than the label. In the case of Moët & Chandon, the important thing is that it is Moët & Chandon. The label is less important but ought to live up to the brand name and be a classic label. It was even observed that Moët &

Chandon would be considered disloyal to its public if it used any other label but the traditional one.

To sum up, this research indicated that image in labelling is mostly created by:

- the brand name;
- respecting tradition;
- using a conservative design; anything extravagant or tricky aroused suspicion.

It does not appear that people pay much attention to the information contained on the label. The first thing they look for is whether the bottle contains *brut* or *brut nature* (although most people are not aware of the differences between the two). *Semi-seco* is more or less rejected at the outset. In addition to the brand name, people sometimes read the label to see what type of *cava* the bottle contains, or its vintage.

Nevertheless, even people who considered themselves 'in the know' were utterly unfamiliar with certain technical details of production.

One final reference to the Moët & Chandon image: one of the participants said that if he were going to buy Moët & Chandon all he needed to know was that it was genuine Moët & Chandon; but if he were going to buy some other brand then he would check far more carefully into its background. No one disagreed with that statement.

Boxes

After the bottles and labels were analysed, a number of boxes were displayed. There was no clear preference as to the boxes. The Moët boxes appeared to be the best liked. The Codorníu box also met with approval and was described as conservative and elegant.

The fact that the name Moët appears in large letters was considered important. The box is used only for gifts and is not considered important otherwise. Since the brand name is an important reason for choosing Moët as a gift, it was felt to be a good thing that the name was clearly visible.

Chandon cava?

We concluded by studying reactions to the idea of a *cava* produced by Chandon. The reactions were varied, demonstrating surprise and even shock. Some of the most important observations were:

- It's a shocking idea. I'd have to try it.
- It would be a *cava* for export as well as for Spain.
- It's their revenge.
- I'd try it out of curiosity.
- It's an aberration.

Most of the discussion centred around the name. It was generally felt that Chandon *cava* was not an appropriate choice. Some people felt that it would be better to call it Moët & Chandon instead of just Chandon because the double names sounded better and because it really would be produced by Moët & Chandon, and Chandon by itself doesn't have any special significance. Calling it Chandon would be like using a secondary brand name. Others, perhaps the majority, felt that it would be better to use any other brand name, followed by the words: '*cava* . . . produced by Moët & Chandon'.

Questions for discussion/suggested tasks

1   What would be the target market for Chandon *cava* in Spain?
2   What should be the concept and the positioning?
3   What decisions would you take in brand name, label and packaging?
4   What are the implications of this strategy for marketing a Moët & Chandon *cava* internationally?
5   What is your assessment of Moët & Chandon's decision to develop a *cava*?

3

SEAT in Europe
A strategy for survival

Jordi Montaña and Maria José Trell

The SEAT case examines a situation in which internationalization is vital to corporate survival. It is an example of a strategy for penetrating the European market, although when it was designed it was also a 'survival' strategy.

The history of SEAT

The automobile industry began generating employment and making a major contribution to Spain's industrial development in the 1950s. SEAT (Sociedad Española de Automóviles de Turismo) was founded in 1950 by the Spanish government with the Instituto Nacional de Industria) (INI) as the major shareholder. The idea was to create a national industry and a fleet of Spanish automobiles and to save foreign currency. SEAT operated as an independent company, manufacturing Fiat's low-cost, fuel-saving vehicles under licence until 1978. The Italian company provided the Spaniards with technology, but did not take part in management.

The first SEAT cars came out of the Barcelona factory in May 1953. In order to ensure that all components were nationally produced, SEAT had had to set up a series of suppliers and furnish them with technical guidance, patents and even capital. Prior to this no automotive components industry had existed in Spain.

The 'Ford Act', passed in 1972, opened the doors to US multinationals like Ford and General Motors, giving Spain increased production capacity and a broader range of available models, and making competition for the domestic market much stiffer than before.

The 1973 oil crisis caused the bottom to fall out of the market, and SEAT started losing money. The automobile industry was hard hit by the crisis, not only because the prices of many of the raw materials used in components manufacture soared, but also, and mainly, because the market declined as a result of higher fuel prices.

SEAT's problems were not limited to those stemming directly from the oil crisis, but were aggravated by the internal developments of Fiat (failure to renew its range of models and the fact that the company was concentrating on its problems in Italy, rather than on what was happening in Spain). SEAT became less and less competitive, embarking on a period of losses that lasted for years.

SEAT's competitiveness declined as the result of a number of factors, among them an unwieldy structure, problems with service and quality, a deteriorating image and, above all, the fact that the market was opening up and more brands were becoming available.

SEAT had originally hoped to be part of the Fiat Group, thus gaining access to new technology, economies of scale and international markets. Under the terms of Fiat's 1979 agreement with INI (Spain's National Institute of Industry), the Italians would be in charge of management and financial operations, while SEAT would reserve 50% of its recently expanded production capacity to provide cars for Fiat distributors throughout Europe (approximately 200,000 cars per year). However, the agreement was never implemented. Nine months later, Fiat pulled out of SEAT.

By March 1980 SEAT's prospects were grim. The affiliation with Fiat had ended and SEAT took its first shaky steps as an independent company.

- It had no technology of its own.
- It had no plans for developing products of its own.
- It had an excessive production capacity and too many employees.
- It had a weak financial structure, and the company was heavily in debt.
- Its export markets had dried up because the company no longer had access to Fiat's distribution network.
- It had no corporate image abroad. Prospective customers were unfamiliar with, and uninterested in, its products.

Faced with a situation like this, SEAT devised a strategic plan designed to consolidate the company as an independent organization with its own line of products and a dealer network in Spain and abroad.

Independence was a key element in the plan, and a great deal had to be done before this could be achieved. Huge investments were required to modernize the company's structure, clean up the financial situation and put it in a position to introduce new products. Were such heavy investments justified in a market with a purchasing capacity of only 500,000 cars per year?

The market base was extremely limited, and SEAT would be very vulnerable if it had to depend exclusively on the domestic market. The instability of the automobile industry was a serious strategic risk. Because cars are durable consumer goods, purchasing decisions could easily be put off for months. The market base would have to be sufficiently broad that a drop in any one market would affect final profits as little as possible.

SEAT's strategy was to go international. With such a small domestic market, this was the only option for survival. Foreign markets would provide a broad market base even though they would not be highly profitable.

But net profits of 1.5–2% in the domestic market would practically cover transport costs for export. Profits would be earned on the domestic market, while export markets would help cover the company's enormous fixed costs. So SEAT decided to go global while still aiming to triumph on the Spanish market.

The European market

Demand for European-built cars dropped 3.5% between 1978 and 1981. The industry suffered from excess capacity, forcing European manufacturers to step up their marketing campaigns in order to protect their volume of sales and market share (see Exhibit 1).

The years 1981–5 were highly competitive. The economic crisis and the large number of automobiles in most European countries meant that new registrations dropped in several markets (see Exhibits 2, 3 and 4).

Europe's six leading manufacturers were: VAG (Volkswagen–Audi), Ford, Fiat (Fiat, Lancia, Autobianchi), Renault, PSA (Peugeot, Talbot, Citroën) and General Motors (Opel, Vauxhall). Between them they accounted for 70% of the EC market. By countries, the leading producers were Germany, France, Italy, Spain and the UK (see Exhibits 5 and 6).

Japanese manufacturers had quickly become a force to be reckoned with. Their share of the EC market had increased by 27% between 1979 and 1981 and by 1985 was almost 11% of the total, although this varied from one country to another, largely due to different entry quotas (see Exhibits 7–11). The major Japanese manufacturers had adopted a strategy of offering better-equipped vehicles at competitive prices.

Meanwhile, product life cycles were becoming shorter and shorter, and this would prove to be a key factor in coming years. While life cycles had been between 7 and 10 years during the 1960s and 1970s, they were now down to around 4 years, and competition was stiffer than ever.

The cost of launching new cars on the market had increased considerably. Design was relatively cheap in comparison to testing and marketing costs. Thus, pay-backs had been cut in half, and heavier investments were necessary. The manufacturers had to meet enormous monthly payments, and the unstable market was thus a danger to survival.

Exhibit 1   *Industrial volume and advertising costs: Western European passenger cars, 1978–81*

	1978	1979	1980	1981
Vehicles (thousands)	10,015	10,330	9,967	9,664
Advertising costs per car sold (pesetas)				
Ford	3,652	5,890	8,360	11,000
General Motors	9,855	10,160	10,780	12,320
VW–Audi	6,389	7,260	9,130	9,350
Renault	6,642	7,380	7,480	8,800
Peugeot	5,426	7,140	12,760	14,190
Citroën	8,024	9,440	11,330	12,430
Talbot	12,202	12,710	17,600	19,580
Fiat	6,139	7,870	8,360	9,130
BL (British Leyland)	9,582	10,530	12,870	13,640
Japanese makes	10,778	15,850	17,600	17,820
Average	7,869	9,423	11,627	12,826

Source: SEAT

Exhibit 2   *Automobile numbers in Europe, 1981–5 (millions of vehicles)*

	1981	1982	1983	1984	1985
West Germany	23.7	24.0	24.7	25.4	26.1
Increase over 1981 (%)	–	1.3	4.2	7.2	10.1
France	19.8	20.3	20.6	20.8	20.9
Increase over 1981 (%)	–	2.5	4.0	5.1	5.6
Italy	18.6	19.6	20.3	20.8	21.3
Increase over 1981 (%)	–	5.4	9.1	11.8	14.5
UK	15.6	16.1	16.6	17.3	17.7
Increase over 1981 (%)	–	3.2	6.4	10.9	13.5
Spain	7.9	8.4	8.7	8.9	9.3
Increase over 1981 (%)	–	6.3	10.1	12.7	17.7
Total EC	88.5	90.9	103.1	105.6	108.0
Increase over 1981 (%)	–	2.7	16.5	19.3	22.0
Total Western Europe	107.6	110.7	113.9	116.6	119.2
Increase over 1981 (%)	–	2.9	5.9	8.4	10.8

Source: DRI, *World Automotive Forecast Report*, November 1986

The drop in pay-backs had to be compensated for by increased efficiency and volume. The economies of scale were becoming globalized.

The EC automobile industry is made up of different categories: A, B, C, D, E, F and G, which are called 'segments' by the manufacturers. The characteristics of the vehicles in each segment differ in terms of specifications (size, design, power, type of engine, etc.) and how the car is

Exhibit 3   *Growth of car ownership in major markets, 1981–5 (automobiles per 1,000 inhabitants)*

Market	1981	1982	1983	1984	1985
West Germany	384	390	402	415	428
Increase over 1981 (%)	–	1.6	4.7	8.1	11.5
France	364	373	376	379	380
Increase over 1981 (%)	–	2.5	3.3	4.1	4.4
Italy	326	346	356	364	372
Increase over 1981 (%)	–	6.1	9.2	11.7	14.1
UK	277	285	295	308	314
Increase over 1981 (%)	–	2.9	6.5	11.2	13.4
Spain	211	219	229	232	241
Increase over 1981 (%)	–	3.8	8.5	10.0	14.2

Source: DRI, *World Automotive Forecast Report*, November 1986

Exhibit 4   *Car registrations in leading European markets, 1981–5 (millions of vehicles)*

Market	1981	1982	1983	1984	1985
West Germany	2,330	2,156	2,427	2,394	2,379
Increase over 1981 (%)	–	−7.5	4.2	2.7	2.1
France	1,835	2,056	2,018	1,758	1,766
Increase over 1981 (%)	–	12.0	10.0	−4.2	−3.8
Italy	1,739	1,684	1,581	1,636	1,746
Increase over 1981 (%)	–	−3.2	−9.1	−5.9	0.4
UK	1,485	1,555	1,792	1,750	1,832
Increase over 1981 (%)	–	4.7	20.7	17.8	23.4
Spain	504	533	547	520	572
Increase over 1981 (%)	–	5.8	8.5	3.2	13.5
Total EC	8,938	9,059	9,492	9,212	9,540
Increase over 1981 (%)	–	1.4	6.2	3.1	6.7
Total Western Europe	9,826	10,012	10,496	10,161	10,608
Increase over 1981 (%)	–	1.9	6.5	3.4	8.0

Source: DRI, *World Automotive Forecast Report*, November 1986

viewed by consumers (compact vehicles, family cars, prestige cars, price, performance, etc.):

- Segment A: compact cars (SEAT Marbella, Fiat Panda, etc.).
- Segment B: small cars (Opel Corsa, Renault 5, etc.).
- Segment C: medium–low range (SEAT Malaga, Opel Kadett).
- Segment D: medium–high range (Ford Sierra, Citroën BX).
- Segment E: large sedans (BMW, Mercedes).
- Segment F: luxury sports cars (Porsche, BMW Serie 7, etc.).
- Segment G: vans (SEAT Terra, VW Kombi, etc.).

Exhibit 5   *Leading automobile manufacturers in Europe,*
1981–5

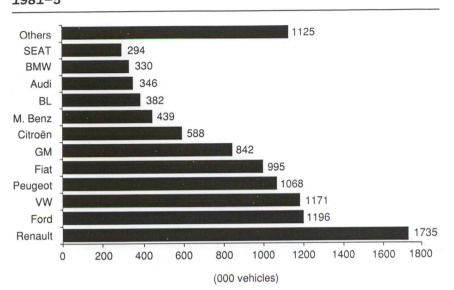

(000 vehicles)

Exhibit 6   *Automobile manufacturers' market share in Europe,*
1981–5 (%)

Manufacturer	1981	1982	1983	1984	1985
VAG	12.8	11.9	11.7	12.0	12.9
Ford	12.2	12.2	12.5	12.8	11.9
Fiat	12.8	12.3	12.1	12.7	12.2
PSA	13.1	12.2	11.7	11.5	11.6
General Motors	8.2	9.5	11.1	11.0	11.3
Renault	13.8	14.5	12.6	10.9	10.7
Japanese makes	9.6	9.5	10.1	10.3	10.8
SEAT	1.4	1.4	1.3	1.5	1.5

Source: DRI, *World Automotive Forecast Report*, November 1986

Exhibit 7   *Automobile manufacturers' shares in West Germany,*
1983–5 (%)

Manufacturer	1983	1984	1985
VAG	28.3	27.9	31.7
Ford	11.9	12.3	10.7
Fiat	4.2	4.6	4.3
PSA	3.8	4.0	4.1
General Motors	18.5	16.3	15.4
Renault	3.7	3.6	3.1
Japanese	10.6	12.0	13.3
SEAT	–	0.2	0.2

Source: DRI, *World Automotive Forecast Report*, November 1986

Exhibit 8 *Automobile manufacturers' market shares in France, 1981–5 (%)*

Manufacturer	1983	1984	1985
VAG	5.7	5.5	6.3
Ford	7.1	7.9	7.5
Fiat	5.1	5.5	5.3
PSA	32.2	33.1	34.7
General Motors	3.8	4.4	4.9
Renault	35.1	31.0	28.7
Japanese	2.7	3.0	3.1
SEAT	0.1	1.0	1.2

Source: DRI, *World Automotive Forecast Report*, November 1986

Exhibit 9 *Automobile manufacturers' market shares in Italy, 1983–5 (%)*

Manufacturer	1983	1984	1985
VAG	5.7	5.9	8.2
Ford	4.6	4.5	4.0
Fiat	55.4	54.3	52.1
PSA	6.4	5.9	6.9
General Motors	3.5	3.2	3.2
Renault	10.2	8.9	10.3
Japanese	0.1	0.1	0.2
SEAT	0.2	1.9	2.1

Source: DRI, *World Automotive Forecast Report*, November 1986

Exhibit 10 *Automobile manufacturers' market shares in the UK, 1983–5 (%)*

Manufacturer	1983	1984	1985
VAG	5.6	5.5	5.7
Ford	28.9	27.8	26.5
Fiat	2.8	2.9	3.1
PSA	5.9	5.4	5.5
General Motors	14.6	16.2	16.6
Renault	3.5	3.4	3.9
Japanese	10.8	11.3	10.9
SEAT	–	–	–

Source: DRI, *World Automotive Forecast Report*, November 1986

Exhibit 11 *Automobile manufacturers' market shares in Spain, 1981–5 (%)*

Manufacturer	1981	1982	1983	1984	1985
VAG	0.8	0.7	1.2	5.5	8.6
Ford	13.8	15.3	13.2	14.6	13.4
Fiat	0.3	0.4	0.7	1.1	1.3
PSA	20.1	17.2	17.0	19.6	17.9
General Motors	0.6	3.1	9.6	9.7	12.0
Renault	32.2	32.2	31.3	28.5	29.9
Japanese	1.4	1.4	1.1	0.7	0.7
SEAT	27.1	26.4	22.6	17.3	12.7

Source: DRI, *World Automotive Market Forecast*, November 1986

Exhibit 12 *Segmentation: Western European market, 1978–81 (%)*

Segment	1978	1979	1980	1981
Segment A	3.5	3.2	2.5	2.3
Segment B	22.5	22.2	24.3	25.7
Segment C	22.7	24.1	28.1	30.9
Segment D	25.0	25.6	23.3	21.2
Segment E	19.0	17.2	14.4	12.7
Segment F	7.3	7.7	7.4	7.2
Total	100.0	100.0	100.0	100.0

Source: DRI, *World Automotive Forecast Report*, 1983

This segmentation by product categories is not always coherent or consistent with market segments (groups ·of consumers) whose needs are similar enough to warrant individualized marketing campaigns (see Exhibits 12 and 13).

Although it may seem that there are few real technological break-throughs in the automobile industry, the truth is that progress is constant in the fields of engine building, materials and mechanical systems.

Cars are machines and as such they are difficult to advertise. Perhaps for this reason cars are marketed today on the basis of their extras, their added technology. What is sold is not technology alone, but 'improved' technology.

The aesthetics of design also play a key role in marketing the leading makes of cars.

Moreover, the reasons for purchasing a particular make or model of car are not always rational, and the emotion or pleasure a car produces is an important element in determining consumer choice, as is 'just because' or 'because I like this one better' reasoning. The key goal in

Exhibit 13 *Market segments: Western European manufactured passenger cars, 1981–5 (000s)*

Manufacturer/segment	1981	1982	1983	1984	1985
Ford Europe					
Segment A	–	–	–	–	–
Segment B	357	328	357	368	344
Segment C	448	478	506	542	527
Segment D	376	384	406	316	336
Segment E	97	89	71	63	101
Total	1,278	1,279	1,340	1,289	1,308
GM Europe					
Segment A	–	–	–	–	–
Segment B	42	44	264	264	277
Segment C	415	438	434	376	537
Segment D	251	414	397	343	348
Segment E	151	150	174	146	123
Total	859	1,046	1,263	1,129	1,285
VW–Audi Group					
Segment A	–	–	–	–	–
Segment B	117	175	166	156	185
Segment C	689	622	597	733	879
Segment D	514	490	480	449	484
Segment E	142	140	212	210	186
Total	1,462	1,427	1,455	1,548	1,734
PSA Group					
Segment A	129	114	74	55	55
Segment B	383	466	460	584	643
Segment C	286	228	170	80	70
Segment D	353	292	514	459	425
Segment E	349	300	279	233	202
Total	1,500	1,400	1,497	1,411	1,395
Fiat Group					
Segment A	272	284	265	234	242
Segment B	197	240	408	482	556
Segment C	367	369	417	461	370
Segment D	151	134	43	12	3
Segment E	46	14	25	17	36
Total	1,033	1,071	1,158	1,206	1,207
Renault Group					
Segment A	173	181	171	125	102
Segment B	505	511	434	337	501
Segment C	345	575	823	709	537
Segment D	399	336	265	184	92
Segment E	80	75	53	119	152
Total	1,502	1,678	1,746	1,474	1,384

Source: SEAT

Exhibit 14 *Perception of cars in general: breakdown by country of origin*

Country of origin	Strong points	Weak points
West Germany	Safety, durability, reliability	Standard accessories, economy, price
France	Comfort, stability	Durability
Italy	Design, performance	Durability
Japan	Standard accessories, price, economy, technology	Durability (more so than Italy and France)

Source: Research Services Ltd, 1985

car advertising is to reflect a lifestyle that is appropriate to the target group.

It is not easy for consumers to choose between cars in the medium- and lower-medium price range. One of the most decisive points is reliability: which car will give me the least trouble? Upkeep is a considerable expense for people in the middle income brackets, so these consumers are looking for quality at a reasonable price. It is easy to choose a car by design, which is something visible, but what about the things you can't see – performance, etc.? That is when national stereo-types come into play: German, French, Scandinavian, Japanese cars. For example, German cars are the best known in Europe and have the strongest image of safety and solid construction. French cars are considered comfortable and inexpensive to maintain. Italian cars are strong on design and handling, but less so than German ones. Japanese cars offer a lot of extras as standard equipment, and the quality/price ratio is good. In many cases, country images are stronger than brand or model images, and the qualities attributed to cars manufactured in a particular country do not vary substantially from one make of car to another (see Exhibit 14).

SEAT on the foreign market

Production, 1980

SEAT had four large factories: Barcelona, Martorell, Prat de Llobregat and Pamplona, with production capacity of over 400,000 cars per year.

The first and largest factory was built in Barcelona's Zona Franca in 1950. By 1980 this occupied 1,260,000 square metres, 730,000 square metres of which was constructed surface. The factory's 33,000 employees could produce 1,700 cars per day.

The Martorell factory occupied 3 million square metres of constructed space and housed the mechanical components plant (brakes, steering columns and suspensions). These components were later assembled in the

Barcelona and Pamplona factories. Adjacent to this was the central spare parts warehouse, which occupied 63,000 square metres and had 420 employees, who distributed spare parts to authorized dealers. Also located in Martorell was the research and development centre, which was created in 1975 for the purpose of carrying out research on how to improve products and update models.

The Prat factory specialized in the production of gears, differentials and gear boxes.

The Pamplona factory occupied 477,000 square metres, 84,000 of which was constructed surface. With 1,500 employees, the factory could produce 400 cars per day, and investments had recently been made in order to increase its capacity.

Commercial situation, 1980

SEAT's position was very shaky. By 1980 SEAT had been operating for thirty years, but it did not yet have its own sales network in Europe. It had always exported through the Fiat network, but when the Italian company pulled out of SEAT, that arrangement came to an end (see Exhibit 15).

Exhibit 15 *SEAT export channels, 1977–82 (number of SEAT vehicles sold through most important networks)*

	1977	1978	1979	1980	1981	1982
Fiat	48,430	66,036	102,443	117,878	78,357	95,200
SEAT	3,561	3,714	6,300	6,702	12,548	14,100

Source: SEAT

SEAT's exports went to a limited number of countries. Andorra, Egypt, Chile, Greece and Cyprus accounted for 80% of the company's exports.

Not only was SEAT without a sales network but it was *unfamiliar with the way the export market operated*, with its distribution channels and with the structure of European markets.

Moreover, *the corporate and brand images* abroad were highly influenced by the former export policy. European consumers were vaguely aware that SEAT existed (they identified it as a subsidiary of Fiat). However, the image of Spanish/Italian cars in Europe was not very competitive. So the main problems were that SEAT did not have an independent brand image known outside of Spain (see Exhibit 16) and that European consumers had little inclination to purchase Spanish-made cars, which were assumed to be poorly finished and not very durable.

Exhibit 16   *What consumers in the major European markets think about Spanish-made vehicles (%)*

Characteristic	West Germany	France	Italy
Fuel savers	16	6	13
Comfortable	10	2	3
Many standard accessories	9	4	6
High performance	5	2	2
Mechanically reliable	13	3	4
Stable	8	3	5
Good design	10	3	5
Value for money	4	7	19

The question asked was: 'Which of the characteristics listed do you feel apply to cars manufactured in Spain?' (% of replies).

Source: Research Services Ltd, 1985

Development strategy

Thus it was that SEAT was led to develop a strategic plan designed to consolidate its independence and build internationally.

First phase of the plan: 1981–5

Strategic objective

1 Guarantee the survival of the SEAT company without breaking completely with Fiat technology

2 Develop a SEAT technology

3 Co-operate with multi-national groups

Strategic actions taken

- Co-operation agreements with Fiat (1981)
- Reduce personnel (1981–4)
- Restructure sales network (1981)

- Introduce SEAT models (1982–3)
- SEAT foreign network (1982)

- Agreements with VW (1982)

The initial strategic plan consisted of four main programmes for action:

Industrial rationalization programme   This programme was designed to cut costs and improve productivity. From 1981 to 1984 manpower was reduced by almost 25%, while production increased from 209,000 cars in 1981 to 279,000 in 1984, an increase of approximately 33%. With this reduction in personnel, productivity levels were expected to reach about 15 cars per employee per year by 1986.

At the same time SEAT aimed to restore discipline and morale in the workforce as an additional way to improve productivity. Co-operation with the labour unions was a key factor in this process.

Alongside the drive to improve productivity and reduce costs, SEAT introduced its first total quality programmes. These programmes were to serve as the basis for the company's future production strategy where quality is now a key objective.

New product development programme   The aim of this programme was to renew the complete range of products, including engines and other important components, in record time. The programme began by introducing new versions of existing SEAT products (models 131, 127, Ritmo and Panda). Since 1981 the renovated Fura and Ronda models have been introduced, along with the Trans van, the Ibiza (1984) and Malaga (1985) models and the new Porsche System engines, fully designed and developed by SEAT (see below).

Technological co-operation programme   The aim of this programme was to reach an agreement with some international group in order to increase the company's capacity and technological know-how. In 1981 collaboration agreements were signed with specialized firms such as Guigiarto, Karmann and Porsche.

In September 1982 a technological-transfer agreement was signed with VW, enabling SEAT to produce 120,000 Volkswagens per year, 50,000 of which were VW Polos to be exported through VW's European network. At that time the Volkswagen–Audi Group was Europe's leader in the manufacture and sale of automobiles and ranked fourth worldwide.

In September 1982 the Industrial Co-operation, Licensing and Technical Assistance Agreement was signed by SEAT and Volkswagen. This agreement did not contain any terms relating to participation in SEAT share capital, but allowed SEAT to produce Volkswagen models Polo/Classic and Passat/Santana/Variant as of 1982. SEAT was able to produce 120,000 of these cars per year using the German technology and making more efficient use of its own manufacturing and sales facilities.

The collaboration arrangements between Volkswagen and SEAT took on a new meaning when the German company decided to buy into SEAT. Before concluding the deal, SEAT undertook a three-stage operation designed to achieve a financial turn-around and adjust the personnel situation. First, the company's accumulated losses at 31 December 1984 were acknowledged on the balance sheet; secondly, SEAT floated a stock issue that increased its net assets to 80 billion pesetas by 31 December 1985; and lastly, the company sold 51% of its shares to VW.

In exchange, VW would undertake to meet the goals set in SEAT's 1981 Strategic Plan, which were to continue producing and selling SEAT automobiles, to maintain the SEAT sales network at home and abroad and to promote the SEAT R&D centre.

This association would provide the advantages of economies of scale in terms of both investments and costs; SEAT and VW–Audi product ranges would complement one another; SEAT would benefit from VW technology; and VW would be able to profit from the SEAT facilities in Spain and from a second distribution channel in Europe.

SEAT thus secured its production levels, and VW was able to take advantage of both the potential Spanish market and lower production costs (the labour factor).

Export network development programme The idea was that this programme would account for 50% of SEAT's installed production capacity, but prospects were not very bright. In May 1981 SEAT and Fiat agreed that as of 1 January 1983 SEAT could update all the Fiat models it had been producing under licence and export them through its own channels. The only exception was the Panda, which Fiat would continue exporting until 1 January 1986.

As part of this agreement Fiat would undertake to export 100,000 cars in 1981 and 1982. From 1983 to 1985 exports would be cut to 45,000 Pandas per year. In 1986 SEAT would make some alterations in the Panda and take over the exports from Fiat.

The primary goal of the export programme was to shift exports from the Fiat network to an international SEAT network which did not as yet exist.

From 1981 to 1985 the market situation was not very promising for SEAT. The domestic market was becoming increasingly competitive: the leading manufacturers had introduced a number of different models aimed at the same market segments that were SEAT's target. Among these models were the Peugeot 205, Ford Orion, Visa, Escort Diesel, R-9, Opel Kadett and Opel Corsa. In addition, customs quotas on the entry of foreign cars had eased up considerably. Opening the borders made competition on the domestic market tougher than ever.

One of SEAT's main objectives was to improve its tarnished corporate image in Spain and make the company known abroad. Up until 1984–5 SEAT had been virtually unknown abroad, which meant that the company had to promote its image before introducing its cars on the European market. The typical SEAT customer came from the lower middle class, was relatively uneducated and chose SEAT because of the price. The company wanted to move up-market to appeal to segments more aware of technology, design and status – qualities usually associated with higher socio-economic groups.

Market research (see Exhibit 17) revealed little intent to purchase SEAT automobiles. In order to improve sales in Europe it was imperative

Exhibit 17 *Extent of desirability: breakdown by country of origin (%)*

Country of origin	West Germany	Netherlands	Belgium	Austria	France	Italy
West Germany	91	72	73	82	59	67
Japan	38	49	55	61	30	19
France	27	35	45	30	78	52
Italy	16	22	23	30	27	89
United Kingdom	8	18	16	11	10	14
Eastern Europe	3	12	12	5	6	4
Spain	4	10	13	8	6	16

The question asked was: 'If a car made in . . . was available in the size and price range you prefer, would you be willing to possibly/definitely buy it?' (% of affirmative responses).

Source: Research Services Ltd, 1985

that SEAT create a clear, distinct and dynamic image. Spanish cars (i.e. SEAT) were much less acceptable than similar cars from other countries, and the rate of acceptance was comparable only to that of Eastern European products. The biggest incentives for buying any SEAT other than the Ibiza model were the price and the standard equipment (value for money). Price was not so important for the Ibiza: technology and style were what counted most.

SEAT aimed to attain a solid position both at home and abroad in order to present a clearer, more coherent image. The strategy it chose was based on the idea of ECONOSPORT, which stressed the following features:

- *Individualism*: range, accessories, personalized features.
- *Economy*: quality, reliability, low maintenance costs, value for money.
- *Sportiness*: design/aesthetics, performance, driving pleasure.

The strategy would sell what were SEAT's strong points at that time:

- *Value for money*: 'El coche mas generoso' (the most generous car).
- *Sport*: IBIZA = Mediterranean, sporty, robust.
- *National characteristics*: pride, fun, vacations = 'Hecho con orgullo, conducido con placer' (produced with pride, driven with pleasure).
- *Creativity and innovativeness*: 'Technologia sin fronteras' (technology without limits).

This strategy quickly increased brand awareness. Meanwhile, exports continued to follow a product- and customer-oriented strategy, offering a limited and exclusive range of models with high-quality accessories.

Market strategy

The strategy for the future was to gain a position in Segments A, B and C of the market.

Product The short- and medium-term goal was to keep the SEAT range fully competitive in terms of price, standard accessories, product range and optional accessories. The long-term aim was to increase the gross margin by increasing the added value and the number of optional accessories per vehicle, developing new lines, new engines and more optional accessories that would add variety to the product range and increase net income per car.

In 1981 and 1982 SEAT introduced the Fura and Ronda models, which were adaptations of Fiat products. The Ronda System Porsche, with the first SEAT-built engine, was introduced in 1983.

Additional SEAT products were launched in 1984 (Ibiza) and 1985 (Malaga). These models no longer used Italian technology.

The scheduled introduction of the SEAT Marbella in 1985 brought the Fiat period to its close. Fiat stopped producing Pandas in Spain. Since 1982 SEAT had been producing its first VW models: VW Polos for the Spanish and export markets and VW Passats exclusively for the domestic market.

Price Prices for each country were set on the basis of average prices of the most similar models available from the competition in that particular country. The SEAT Ronda was priced at 98% of the resulting average while the Ibiza was priced at 100%. Prices varied in each specific market according to the existing competition and SEAT's aimed-for market penetration.

Brand and product image SEAT aimed to develop an independent, modern and dynamic brand and product image through promotional campaigns, participation in public events and programmes designed to reach the customer and make SEAT products and dealers widely known within a short period of time.

Marketing plans were developed jointly by importers and the SEAT export division and were regularly revised and expanded in accordance with the particular economic situation in each market.

After-sales service SEAT also aimed to establish a high-quality service network that would quickly solve customer problems and provide service that would be commensurate with the brand image the company wanted to promote.

Service is an extremely important, but often neglected, part of corporate image. SEAT emphasized the importance of its after-sales service, using feedback from this to improve its quality and brand image.

Special care was taken in selecting and training dealers. Most dealerships went to proprietors of family-owned garages, who already worked largely with service and repairs.

Export network development programme

The main objectives for the period were:

* To export 36,400 vehicles in 1983, 59,300 in 1984, 78,300 in 1985 and 105,800 in 1986; this would give SEAT a 1% share of the European market (see Exhibit 18).
* To export Rondas and Furas in 1983, Ibizas in the autumn of 1984, Malagas in the summer of 1985 and Marbellas in the autumn of 1986.
* When exports through Fiat began dropping off, SEAT decided to start producing for the export market in 1983. This meant that the first contracts with importers had to be signed by the end of February 1983.

Establishing an export network was a difficult task. SEAT had no importers or dealers outside of Spain except in Chile, Lebanon, Egypt, Cyprus and Greece. SEAT was virtually unknown in the major European

Exhibit 18   *Sales targets for SEAT products, 1983–7*

Country	1983	1984	1985	1986	1987
Andorra	150	250	250	250	250
Austria	1,250	1,700	2,220	1,750	1,478
Belgium	2,400	3,100	4,360	5,320	7,360
Chile	2,400	2,700	2,800	–	–
Denmark	–	450	750	1,450	829
Finland	–	730	1,130	2,220	1,542
France	8,550	10,500	15,470	23,820	25,153
Germany (West)	10,250	13,350	16,300	6,830	7,415
Greece	1,000	1,200	1,400	1,700	4,011
Ireland	–	–	–	670	704
Israel	–	–	–	1,250	2,790
Italy	7,300	14,000	17,350	35,830	57,622
Netherlands	2,750	3,550	4,780	7,370	7,481
Norway	–	440	630	–	–
Portugal	–	–	–	940	2,969
Sweden	–	600	880	–	–
Switzerland	–	1,330	2,130	3,410	3,498
Taiwan	–	–	–	3,670	2,503
UK	–	–	–	8,260	9,114
Others	350	5,400	7,850	1,060	396
Total	36,400	59,300	78,300	105,800	135,115

Source: SEAT

markets or else believed to be a Fiat subsidiary. Furthermore, little or nothing was known about Spanish industry or its capacity to produce cars. European consumers generally had no idea what to expect of Spanish cars but assumed that workmanship and durability would be poor and were not about to consider buying one.

Phases of the export programme

Export market development plan World markets were analysed, as were the policies and standards applied by the competition. This helped SEAT decide on its export targets. During the first phase of the programme, the company concentrated on the main European markets in order to increase volume and profit margins as much as possible. At the same time, markets in the Americas, the Far East, Africa and Asia were gradually developed.

The European export plan aimed to take advantage of the huge potential market in Europe. The first steps were to develop the sales network in Europe, position SEAT and its products in European markets and create an efficient sales organization that would enable the company to set up and maintain the necessary programmes for achieving its export goals.

Target countries for market development strategy were divided into three categories, depending upon ease of entry (import legislation and local driving habits), total market volume, potential gross margins, the existence of market segments suitable for SEAT products and the penetration of Fiat (familiarity with Fiat made SEAT easier to sell).

The first markets to be developed were West Germany, Belgium, Luxembourg, the Netherlands, Andorra, Austria, France and Italy (1983), followed by Denmark, Norway, Switzerland and Finland (1984). Great Britain and Ireland were left until 1985 when SEAT models would be available with right-hand drive.

In 1982 there were only two models available for export: the Fura (the first car to be exported in this new period of SEAT's development), which was launched in the Netherlands, and the Ronda Full Equip. The other models available in Spain were produced under licence from Fiat and could not be exported.

Even with a single product, there were problems: Fiat took SEAT to court in Paris, charging that the changes SEAT had made in the product (as per agreements between the two companies) were not enough to differentiate the SEAT model significantly from the Fiat Ritmo. SEAT won the case and was able to put its export plan into motion, having gained a certain 'notoriety' which was helpful in a market where SEAT was virtually unknown.

In September 1982 SEAT began opening its first eight target markets in other countries, selecting importers and launching a campaign to attract dealers. In selecting importers a great deal of attention was paid

Exhibit 19   *SEAT's export market development, 1983–7*

	Export sales points (total network)	Importers	Points of sale (total Europe)
1983	552	9	509
1984	1,156	24	1,061
1985	1,644	28	1,516
1986	2,167	28	2,046
1987	2,517	31	2,356

		Europe		Italy		France	
	Total	Dealers	Agents	Dealers	Agents	Dealers	Agents
1983	509	509	–	99	–	69	–
1984	1,061	997	64	175	–	169	–
1985	1,516	1,344	172	217	–	174	–
1986	2,046	1,383	663	226	180	180	201
1987	2,356	1,478	878	241	321	188	240

Source: SEAT

to management and organization skills, dealer network, financial solvency, etc. (see Exhibit 19).

Representation, marketing and after-sales service policies As already mentioned, the European market was highly competitive. Following several years of crisis, the leading car manufacturers had stepped up their marketing efforts, investing more in advertising, promotion and special offers and continually introducing new models.

SEAT needed to get results fast in order to meet its operating goals and assure that the foreign sales network would be profitable. The aim was to set up a strong, extensive and profitable SEAT network in the short and medium term with the long-term objective of participating directly in the European markets through subsidiaries or fully owned SEAT companies.

SEAT created a sales organization to deal exclusively with the export market (see Exhibit 20). This was a very small outfit, composed of a central team and several operating divisions. Sales offices were set up in the principal areas of operation.

Because the company had limited means at its disposal, the strategy was to use importers' facilities (offices, equipment, etc.). This kept costs down and enabled SEAT to start operating quickly.

The importers concentrated on setting up the first network of dealers, while SEAT designed a complete introductory plan, which included definitions of its product, price and communications policies:

Exhibit 20 Organization: SEAT's export markets department

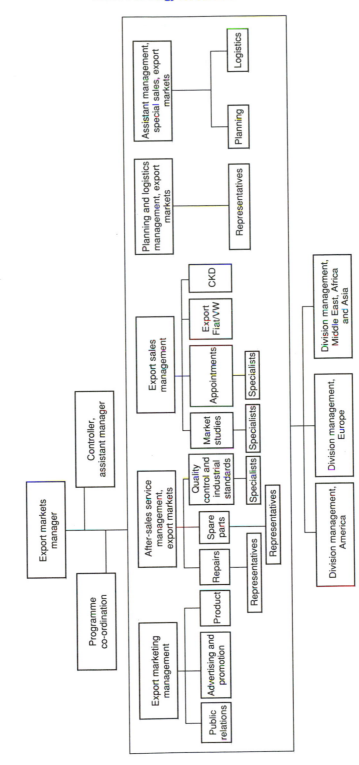

Exhibit 21   *Updated export plan*

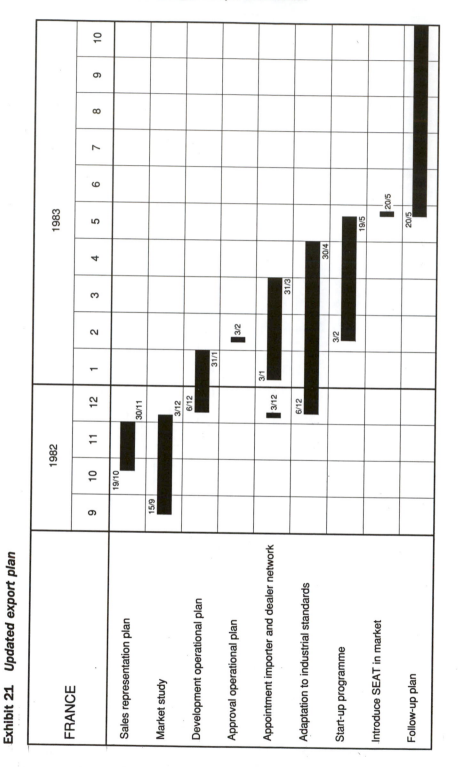

- three-year volume plan;
- pricing policy based on individual market situations;
- standard equipment policy, based on an analysis of the competition and designed to offer a better-equipped product.

See Exhibit 21.

Import contracts contained a very detailed description of the support SEAT would give its importers. Although the importers' margins were similar to those offered by other brands, SEAT offered special marketing support (selling Spain = tourism, folklore, sunshine) and placed special emphasis on public relations (good contacts with the press, special presentation of the Ibiza model for the 'car of the year' jury, etc.).

Conclusion

Juan José Díaz Ruiz, SEAT's export sales manager, is talking to some other SEAT executives:

It was like having a blank map of the world in front of us and only a short time to fill it all in. We had to make an unknown company from a misunderstood country into an attractive and credible proposition. We had to interest importers, dealers and particularly the broad international market. We had to make SEAT, a Spanish car, a totally acceptable and attractive purchase alternative in tremendously competitive markets in Europe and elsewhere.

Now, in 1985, we are starting on the second phase of our expansion into the rest of Europe and other markets: Switzerland in February, the Scandinavian countries between May and July, the UK and Ireland in October. What's more, as of February 1985 we are the number 1 imported car in Taiwan and we will soon be moving into other markets in that area. We hope that this expansion will enable us to export 116,700 cars and increase the number of SEAT dealers to 1,450 by the end of 1985. In 1986 we plan to consolidate operations in the rest of the world and hope to increase exports to 167,000 cars and dealers to 2,180.

Questions for discussion/suggested tasks

1 Analyse SEAT's position in 1982. What were the main problems?
2 Which of the steps taken during 1980–5 are key factors affecting SEAT's likely success? What strategic alternatives would you propose for the future?
3 Explain SEAT's positioning in the European market. Evaluate the ECONOSPORT concept as an appropriate basis for SEAT's positioning.
4 Define a new product concept and the most appropriate type of product. Develop a positioning proposal.
5 Devise a plan for breaking into the European market.

4

Nescafé Italy
Global brand, local culture

Michele Costabile and Maria Carmela Ostillio
with Enrico Valdani

One of the most important themes in international marketing is the impact on company marketing of the internationalization or globalization of products and markets. In general it is possible to distinguish between 'multi-domestic' approaches, consisting of adaptation to the particular conditions of each market, and 'global' approaches based on international product or brand standardization. Even a broadly successful 'global' approach can face particular challenges and difficulties in a specific market-place which has a strong and distinctive natural culture that is resistant to the prevailing international brand concept.

The history of Nescafé in the Italian market represents just such a situation. The strong coffee-consumption culture in Italy is one which has not, up till now, been highly receptive to the concept of Nescafé instant coffee. In this case study, Nestlé Italy needs to develop a strategy to address this problem.

Giorgio Baruffa, product manager for Nescafé in Italy, was considering the future market strategy options for the product. Nescafé had been in the Italian market-place for thirty years, yet it had never quite 'made it'. A recent test to increase market share by cutting the price by 20% had not met the objectives, though it had resulted in a 25% increase in sales. Moreover, in the test area follow-up research had shown that the price reduction had weakened consumer perceptions of Nescafé's high-quality image, which, despite everything, the brand had been able to build.

Mr Bechi, marketing director of Nestlé Italy, had therefore decided, along with Mr Baruffa, to call a meeting to analyse the product's problems and to arrive at a consensus decision regarding the future strategy for Nescafé in Italy over the next years. By 1989, in fact, 'a new era for Nescafé has to begin', Mr Bechi said.

The people involved in the meeting, besides the marketing director, were the chief financial officer, the head of strategic planning and Mr Baruffa with his assistant.

Company background: Nestlé

Nestlé SA, headquartered in Switzerland, is one of the world's leading industrial groups. In 1988 Nestlé with 160,000 employees and $20 billion of annual revenues, operated on five continents, producing, in 362 plants, products which reflected consumer tastes in each country.

The company had a decentralized organizational structure within which the operating companies have considerable autonomy in establishing long-term policies, adapting these, of course, to local conditions. This structure takes the form of a 'confederation of companies' comprising 200 operating firms of various sizes and profit contributions.

Of the 160,000 employees in 1988, 43% were based in Europe, 23% in North America, 19% in South America and the remaining 15% in Asia, Africa and Australia. Contribution to total revenues by country were as follows: USA 25%, France 12%, West Germany 11%, Japan 6%, UK 4%, Brazil 4%, Spain 4%, Italy 2%, Switzerland 2% and others 30%.

From its original starting-point with infant food products, including Nestlé powdered milk and condensed milk, the company has undertaken a policy of growth through expansion and diversification. Diversification has been both internal, by creating and launching new products, and external, through merger with and acquisition of companies even outside the food sector.

The implementation of this strategy has led to the launching or selling of numerous products. Among these are chocolate (with such well-known brand names as Gala and Frigor, instant coffee (with the Nescafé and Taster's Choice brands), other instant beverages (the most famous being Nesquik), bouillon cubes and instant soup (brand name Maggi), preserves and fruit juices. Beyond the food sector, Nestlé also operates in the pharmaceutical, cosmetics and hotel industries.

Nestlé is the world's leading producer of instant coffee; it is also the major buyer of raw coffee. The concept of instant coffee was born in the 1930s when stocks far exceeded demand. Overproduction and excess stocks of raw coffee led to the search for an optimum method by which coffee could be preserved in concentrated and soluble form while retaining its flavour.

Nescafé's launch in 1938, just before the Second World War, resulted in rapid diffusion. Nescafé was adopted by all the armed forces involved in the conflict because of its ease and convenience of use. Consumption of instant coffee quickly spread throughout the world.

Instant powdered coffee is obtained through a dehydration process and then packaged in a controlled environment. Granular coffee is derived through the lyophilization method. The final product is packaged in a controlled environment in order to retain both its flavour and aroma.

By 1988 the world drank more than 170 million cups of Nescafé a day. The advertising budget to promote Nescafé worldwide amounted to 350 million Swiss francs annually, and its market share of total coffee consumption ranged from between 10% and 30% in its various markets throughout the world.

Nestlé Italy

Nestlé Italy is a Milan-based company operating in more than ten different industries. Its product portfolio includes over eighty products, generating around $2 billion of revenues annually.

In the Italian market Nestlé has market-share leadership in the categories of milk modifiers (in 1988 Nesquik had a 72% market share of cocoa-based modifiers, and Orzoro had a 63% market share of orzo-based modifiers) and instant coffee (Nescafé had a 80% market share of instant coffee).

In Italy the blends of Nestlé coffee were sold under the brand names Nescafé Classic, Nescafé, Gran Aroma and Nescafé Relax (a decaffeinated coffee). Nescafé sales (Exhibit 1) amounted to around $30 million a year,

Exhibit 1   *Nescafé volume sales ex factory, 1975–88 (tonnes)*

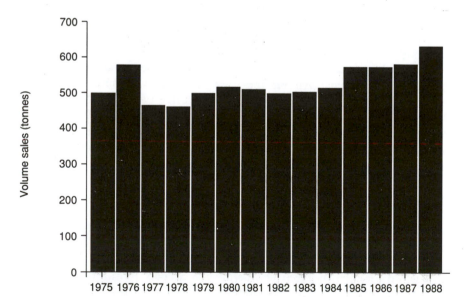

Source: Nestlé Italy

equal to 1.5% of Nestlé Italy's total revenues. In volume Nescafé sales were 500 tonnes in 1982, 580 in 1986 and 650 in 1988.

The main marketing expenditures on the Nescafé brands were on above-the-line advertising (about 5% of the total advertising investment made by Nestlé in Italy), and sales promotion (2% of consumer and trade promotion by Nestlé in Italy). Instant coffee contributed 8% to the Nestlé Italy Beverages Division revenues and 19% to its net profits.

The Italian consumer – key trends

During the 1980s the percentage of food consumed 'away from home' in Italy increased significantly ('home' food consumption grew by 450%, and 'away-from-home' by 700%, in the decade 1978–88).

Among the most important socio-economic changes affecting such developments have been the spread of working hours that include a lunch break, the increasing number of women in the workforce and the ever-increasing number of one-member family units (15% of the total in 1988).

Other evident socio-demographic changes included a reduction in average family size, a differently structured population (higher levels of education; a lower birth rate of 1.7 children per family; ageing of the population), a concentration of shopping in large stores, increased 'personal' involvement in consumption, a greater awareness of the health aspects of diet and a greater sensitivity to ecological problems.

Alongside the above there has been a growing trend towards the consumption of fresh, genuine products, especially among young people with average or higher education (fruit and vegetable consumption increased by 11.6% in the 1986–8 period).

The following are the most significant socio-demographic trends affecting consumption patterns:

1 The increased percentage of senior citizens as a proportion of the total population, with increased disposable income (from an average of 1,250,000 lire per month in 1983 to 1,950,000 in 1988).[1] Demographic forecasts confirm the trend, as shown in Exhibit 2.

2 The increased number of women in the workforce (over 30% of the total female population and *circa* 50% of the female active population in 1988) and consequent increase in food consumption outside the home, as well as increased demand for ready-to-eat and frozen dishes.

3 Increased international mobility both into and out of the country, leading to a greater internationalization of consumer behaviour, especially with respect to durable consumer goods (in the 1980s more than 2 million Italians went abroad each year, and in 1988 this figure reached 3 million, equal to 6% of the population).

4 Changes in the ethnic composition of the population as a result of immigration from Northern Africa and Central Asia (ethnic-minority numbers rising from 150,000 to over 500,000 between 1985 and 1987).

Exhibit 2   Italy's population, by age groups, 1987–97 (%)

Age group	1987	1992	1997 (forecast)
0–14	18.3	15.9	15.2
15–24	16.5	15.4	13.2
25–34	14.2	15.8	16.4
35–44	13.1	13.6	14.2
45–54	12.6	12.5	12.8
55–69	15.6	16.9	17.1
70 and above	9.7	9.9	12.2

Sources: ISTAT (Istituto Nazionale di Statistica) and Censis

5   A rising level of education and culture among the population (in 1988 college graduates made up 6% of the population, those with a high-school qualification 20%, those who finished junior high school 34%, and those with only elementary school education 40%; in 1980 the respective percentages were 3%, 13%, 26% and 56%, with a level of illiteracy equal to 1% of the population).

There have also been considerable change in the consumption of some categories of beverages. In the five years 1983–8 consumption of non-alcoholic beverages increased by about 30%, specifically mineral water (+35%), soft drinks (+32%) and fruit juices (+40%).

Coffee consumption: Italy compared with other countries

Ever since the Arabs discovered the roasting process, towards the end of the fourteenth century, the dark brew that we call coffee has had both a private and a public life. Coffee was, and it still is, tied to the intimacy of the family and home in the first instance, but its public consumption has become enriched by both social and cultural activities connected to it.

Thus coffee-houses, where coffee was typically served, used to be patronized by the most cultured people in literature and knowledge, sustaining their poetical or political dissertations with the stimulus of the aromatic beverage. Coffee-houses were, in fact, once called 'schools of knowledge'.

Venetian merchants first introduced coffee to Italy around 1615, and it was no coincidence that the first coffee-house to open was in Venice. In 1720 the Caffè alla Veneziana Triofante was inaugurated; it later became the Caffè Florian and was regularly patronized by such persons as Lord Byron, Jean-Jacques Rousseau and Silvio Pellico. Coffee-houses have often continued to be places where journalists, artists, actors and others meet, work, pass by, debate and argue.

A wide variety of blends, degree of roasting, methods of preparing and habits of consuming coffee can be found in different countries. Each nation has adapted coffee to its culture and traditions, in particular to its traditional forms of nutrition and food consumption. Thus in certain countries coffee is consumed not only for its stimulating properties, but also as a thirst-quencher; in other parts of the world it is drunk with very little water, as if it were an 'elixir'.

The highest per capita consumption occurs in Northern Europe. In 1988 Sweden/Norway had the highest consumption, with 12 kg per capita annually, followed by Denmark with 11 kg, the Netherlands with 9 kg, Belgium and Austria with 8 kg, West Germany with 7 kg and France and Switzerland with 6 kg. In the United States consumption was about 4.6 kg per person annually, although this figure was much higher in the 1970s. In Italy, where most people perceive themselves to be heavy consumers of coffee, the level of consumption is equal to that of Canada, about 4.3 kg per year. Consumption reduces to about 2 kg per person annually in Greece, the former Yugoslavia, Spain, Great Britain, Australia and Japan. This is the level of coffee consumption in Hungary, while in other Eastern European countries average per capita consumption is less than 1 kg per year.

There is a close relationship between levels of consumption and methods of preparation. In Northern Europe, where the 'filter' method is widespread, consumption is high. This is probably due to the considerable volume of water used in preparing coffee, allowing the beverage to function as a thirst-quencher.

In fact, in most Nordic countries it is quite common to sit down to a meal with a large cup of coffee. It is unusual to drink filtered coffee by itself. Normally it accompanies a hearty breakfast in the morning, while in the afternoon it is usually taken with a slice of pie, pastry or biscuits. Those who drink 'espresso' or 'turkish' coffee, instead, normally drink it with food only at breakfast.

The capacity of coffee cups used also differs. In the Netherlands, for example, the capacity is similar to that of a soft-drink can, while elsewhere it is more like a tumbler.

Corresponding to the different 'cultures' of coffee are the diverse ways in which it can be prepared. There are two principal methods by which the coffee can be extracted from ground coffee beans: soaking or percolation. In the first method, ground coffee is first put into boiling water and allowed to 'soak' for at least five minutes, before the mixture is strained through a filter. In percolation, a flow of boiling water passes through the ground coffee either by its own weight (gravity), similar to the filter method or the method used in 'Neapolitan' coffee pots, or by a light steam pressure, a method employed in 'mocha' coffee pots, or by high pressure (9–10 atmospheres) produced either mechanically or hydraulically by an espresso coffee machine.

There are also significant differences in the levels of caffeine per cup:

Exhibit 3   *The coffee market in Italy, summary, 1988*

Number of companies	750
Number of workers	7,200
Value of production	1,981
(factory prices – billion lire)	
Production share – first 4 companies	41.9%
(value)	
Production share – first 8 companies	52.0%
(value)	
Forecasts for the expansion of production	
1988–9	2–3%
Medium-term trends	1–2%

Source: Databank

60–130 mg per cup when using a mocha coffee pot or espresso machine, 90–125 mg per cup using the filter (percolator) method (particularly common in the USA), 40–100 mg for instant coffee and 2–5 mg for decaffeinated coffee.

Instant coffees, which achieve a significant share of total coffee consumption worldwide, occupy only a small niche of the market in Italy: less than 2% of the total coffee market in 1988. This compared with 8% in the Netherlands, 10% in West Germany, 30% in France, 34% in the USA, 37% in Spain, 51% in Greece, 78% in Portugal and over 90% in the UK and Ireland.

The dynamics of coffee consumption in Italy are affected by the socio-cultural differences between the North and the South, and between every single region of the country. There are, for example, big differences between North and South in cultural attitudes (Northern Italy is more cosmopolitan and 'European'), affluence (Southern Italy is considered one of the less developed regions of the EC) and climate (much more warm and dry in the South). This also reflects food consumption patterns.

The wide range of tastes and preferences has led to a large number of small and medium-size importers and *torrefattori* (coffee roasters) who satisfy demand at the local level in each region. In Italy over 80% of the companies are small firms operating on a local level (see Exhibit 3).

Coffees shipped to Southern Italy are usually stronger, with a higher percentage of Robusta (one of the two main coffee plant types – much stronger and more bitter and less flavoured than Arabica, the other type, while in the North the aroma of the coffee is particularly important.

In Italy the typical coffee drinker is between 15 and 55 years old. In 1988 the highest level of consumption was by the 45–54 age bracket (see Exhibit 4).

Consumer research has shown that some younger and more health-oriented consumers perceive coffee as a 'risky' beverage and try to reduce their consumption.

Coffee has always been regarded, by Italians, as a digestive or

Exhibit 4   *Coffee drinking in Italy, by age group*

Age group	% who usually drink coffee	Annual per capita consumption (kg)	% of total consumption
15–24	50	3.04	12.4
25–34	70	4.36	20.5
35–44	81	4.60	23.0
45–54	83	4.90	24.0
55–69	67	3.13	15.1
70 and above	60	1.86	5.0

Source: A.C. Nielsen Italy

stimulating beverage. Per capita consumption in coffee-houses is the highest in Europe and accounts for about 20% of all the coffee consumed in the entire country. The consumption of coffee in Italy can be characterized in terms of the existence of two large segments of consumers: those who drink coffee at home, and those who drink it in coffee-houses or restaurants.

Just how important coffee is, as a staple of the national diet, can be seen by changing the units of measure, going from kilos to value in lire. Assuming an average quantity of coffee per cup of 6 grams, the Italian market amounted to 35 million cups of coffee (around 600 cups of coffee per person annually). Total retail coffee sales amounted to 11 billion lire (about 192,450 lire per person). Expenditure on coffee is a significant component of the average food budget each year.

The coffee industry in Italy: structure and evolution

Coffee is the largest commodity market in the world. In this market, two competing interests come into play. On the one hand, there is strong competition on price and quantity among producers of raw coffee; on the other, there are different commercial and technological needs among the world manufacturers.

The stability of the market is frequently undermined by the need for foreign exchange on the part of the developing countries that are the producers of raw coffee, which attempt to increase production, causing fluctuations in prices.

Coffee-processing technology differs according to the type of coffee being made: roasted (normal), decaffeinated and instant (soluble).

Coffee companies sell coffee to the following groups of customers: families, coffee-houses, hotels and restaurants. In the 'family' segment, competition is fierce among the companies marketing nationally. Their strategies focus on:

- intensive advertising to enhance the brand image;

- a growing orientation towards modern distribution channels (super-markets, etc.);
- strong promotion at points of sale;
- segmentation of the market according to the quality, price and specific use of coffee.

In the coffee-house, hotel and restaurant ('CHR') segment, competition is primarily between a limited number of companies which operate nationally. However, there were still many small firms which operate on either a regional or a provincial level.

Information on segment dimensions, market shares and the positioning of the major companies in the two different segments are illustrated in Exhibits 5–8.

The dominant positions of firms in these two main segments differ, but the companies which offer a good product in the CHR segment will probably do the same in the family one.

Industry structure

In 1988 the Italian coffee industry comprised about 750 companies, employing 7,200 workers. The first four companies' market share was approximately 42% of the total (52% for the first eight), and 1988 sales at factory prices were $1.5 billion (see Exhibits 5, 6 and 7 for leading companies' market share and for retail sales data). Sales volume was expected to grow at the rate of approximately 2% per year.

The fragmented structure of the industry results from low entry barriers. Only in the purchasing of raw coffee do the larger companies gain advantages from economies of scale, being large enough to buy directly in the foreign countries.

In recent years many companies had been pushed out of the market as a result of competitive pressure (coming especially from market leaders) and the price volatility of raw coffee; this makes it even more important to realize economies of scale in purchases. Exhibit 9 shows the structure of the coffee industry in Italy.

Marketing strategies of the leading companies

The companies in the Italian coffee market employ a range of different marketing policies in terms of product, price, place and promotion.

Coffee is sold in two main forms: either as whole coffee beans or as ground coffee. The former is used in coffee-houses, while the latter is used mainly at home. All of the major firms have a broad range of products with different prices and sizes. Some companies buy instant or decaffeinated coffee from other firms in order to offer a complete product line under their own brand name.

Most recent innovations in the coffee market have focused on the packaging and blends offered. In terms of packaging, there are several

Exhibit 5 Italian coffee market, retail sales, 1988

	Family segment (% on row)				CHR segment (% on row)				Total (% on column)			
	Volume (000 tonnes)	%	Value (billion lire)	%	Volume (000 tonnes)	%	Value (billion lire)	%	Volume (000 tonnes)	%	Value (billion lire)	%
Normal	144.9	69.0	2,105	20.3	65.1	31.0	8,267	79.7	210.1	96.7	10,372	94.5
Decaf.	2.9	58.0	48	10.3	2.1	42.0	410	89.7	5.2	2.3	457	4.2
Instant	1.3	87.5	69	48.9	0.8	12.5	72	51.1	2.1	1.0	141	1.3
Total	149.1	68.6	2,222	20.3	68.0	31.4	8,749	79.7	217.5	100.0	10,970	100.0

Source: Databank

Exhibit 6 Normal roasted coffee: Italian market shares of main producers, 'family' and 'CHR' segment, 1988

	Family				CHR			
	Quantity (000 tonnes)	(%)	Value (billion lire)	(%)	Quantity (000 tonnes)	(%)	Value (billion lire)	(%)
Lavazza	42.0	30.7	405	34.0	3.0	6.5	35	8.6
Procter & Gamble	12.3	9.0	108	9.2	–	–	–	–
Café do Brasil	10.2	7.4	83	7.1	0.5	1.1	4	0.8
Segafredo	4.4	3.2	37	3.2	4.3	9.4	45	8.6
Sao Café	7.0	5.1	58	5.0	–	–	–	–
Illy Caffè	0.4	0.3	6	0.5	1.5	3.2	30	5.6
Total market	137.0		1,170		45.7		520	

Exhibit 7   *Instant coffee: Italian market shares of main producers, 1988*

	Quantity		Value	
	(000 tonnes)	(%)	(billion lire)	(%)
Nestlé	650	77.7	35	80.0
Crippa & Berger	110	13.1	7	15.9
Others	76	9.2	2	4.1
Total	836	100	44	100.0

Exhibit 8   *Italian coffee market strategic groups*

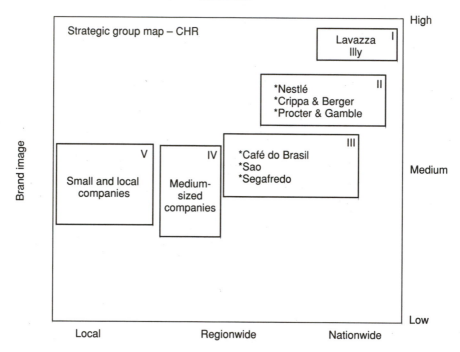

sizes available: 200 and 250 gram bags (49% volume share in the family segment), 400 and 500 gram bags (38%), 500 gram tins (4%) and 1 kg bags (9%). Coffee-shops, hotels and restaurants (CHR) most commonly use 1 kg and 3 kg bags. Instant coffees are available in small glass jars weighing 50–125 grams.

The use of these different-sized packages depends on the type of consumption, the type of coffee and the type of sales channel.

The most frequently used package is the pliable bag, partly because of the relatively low cost of its raw materials, paper and a plastic film used

Exhibit 9   *Structure of the Italian coffee industry*

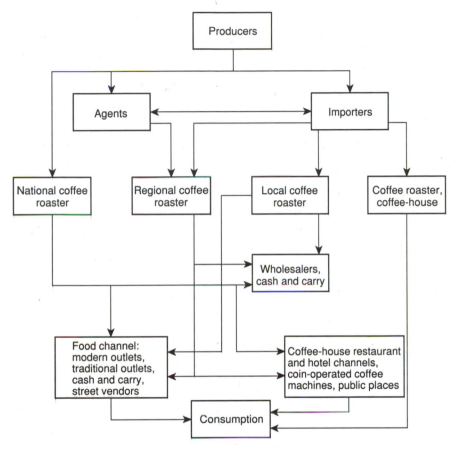

to cover it, the convenience which it offers (lighter package, less bulky) and, in part, the variety of different sizes in which it comes. Looking at Exhibit 10, it is possible to understand the presence of major firms in the distribution channels. This shows the average number of items that major companies have in the different outlet categories, and the numerical and weighted distribution indexes, mainly used by product and brand managers in the grocery markets.

Among the key success factors in modern distribution outlets are the brand image, the sizes offered and the product's display. Yet if the brand name was important for selling coffee to the family segment, then service is the key for selling to the CHR one. Market share in traditional outlets, more and more supplied by wholesalers, have continually declined.

There are many coffee roasters who have made agreements with operators in the CHR segment including forms of financing and discounts on the use of coffee machines as incentives to maintain customer franchises.

Exhibit 10 *Distribution of major companies, October 1988*
(% and average number of items)

	Hypermarkets		Supermarkets		Convenience stores	
	(%)	(av.)	(%)	(av.)	(%)	(av.)
Nestlé	100.0	5.7	100.0	7.2	100.0	6.1
Lavazza	100.0	12.2	100.0	11.1	95.5	10.9
Crippa & Berger	100.0	5.5	100.0	5.4	95.5	3.6
Segafredo	69.6	3.9	60.7	3.9	9.1	2.0
Procter & Gamble	100.0	5.9	94.6	5.9	95.5	4.7
Café do Brasil	30.4	2.2	8.9	3.0	25.5	1.5
Sao Café	69.6	4.5	70.5	4.5	40.5	3.0
Illy Caffè	10.5	2.0	15.7	2.0	5.5	1.0

Distribution analysis: numerical and weighted

	Numerical	Weighted volume index (Nestlé = 100)
Lavazza	73	90
Procter & Gamble	65	77
Crippa & Berger	23	70
Nestlé	70	100
Sao Café	28	60
Café do Brasil	18	30

Source: Nestlé Italy

Given the high-quality coffee obtained through the espresso method and the image of 'coffee-house' coffee, a brand presence in the CHR segment can contribute to its image in the family segment. This is due to the widely held belief that coffee made in a coffee-house is better than the coffee made at home; therefore, consumers are often willing to buy the brands found in coffee-houses.

The average national price for a kilo of roasted (normal) coffee, for operators in the CHR segment, was in 1988 about 18,000 lire (VAT included), but there was a wide variance around the average. This price increased by up to seven or eight times for the end consumer, usually paying 800–900 lire for a 6 gram cup of coffee-shop espresso.

The average national wholesale price for a kilo of roasted coffee is far lower in the family segment (in 1988 around 11,000 lire), while the average price per kilo for decaffeinated or instant coffee is much higher (30,000 lire the decaffeinated and 50,000 lire the instant).

By observing the cost structure of firms operating in the market, it becomes apparent that raw materials (coffee beans) represent about 70% of total costs; packaging material account for 13%; advertising and promotional activities for 2%; wages, depreciation and gross operating profits represent 15%. Breaking down the price of a cup of coffee, the

Exhibit 11 *Coffee advertising investment for the main producers, 1987–8*

	Advertising investment (billion lire)		% of sales	
	1987	1988	1987	1988
Lavazza	34.0	62.0	6.8	11.8
Procter & Gamble	22.6	40.4	18.3	36.2
Nestlé	7.4	4.3	9.1	5.6
Café do Brasil	9.4	18.0	10.1	20.3
Sao Café	3.5	1.3	5.2	2.3
Segafredo	4.3	9.5	4.6	9.4
Crippa & Berger	7.6	13.2	15.2	28.3
Illy Caffè	6.0	7.4	15.9	16.8

Exhibit 12 *Division of advertising investment for the major companies, 1988*

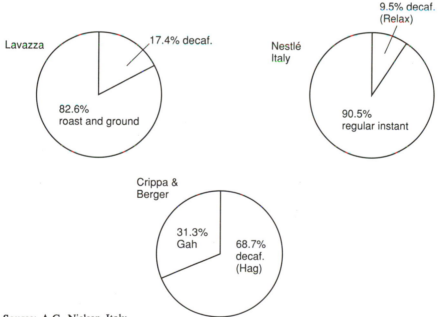

Source: A.C. Nielsen Italy

values are approximately as follows: cost of the blend 15%, cost of sugar 2%, cost of labour 52%, overheads 24% and VAT 6%.

Price is used as a competitive tool when contracting with intermediaries less susceptible to quality, service and promotional policies to differentiate the market.

Advertising, along with distribution, has an important function within the market-place (see Exhibits 11 and 12). In the family segment, market leaders benefit from economies of scale not only in distribution, but also in communications in order to maintain their leadership.

Of total 1988 advertising expenditures, about 77% was on roast and ground coffees, about 21% on decaffeinated and 2% on instant.

Some of the bigger companies exploited one particular brand name as a 'brand umbrella'. This was done, for example, by focusing advertising campaigns on one particular product, e.g. Lavazza Club, and, as a result of the association, promoting the various other Lavazza products.

Sales promotion was another communication tool usually used for the intermediaries of the family and CHR segments. Among the various forms of promotion were: billboards, brochures, signs both in the store and in store windows, and displays which show some originality in presenting the product. Besides these forms of promotion, there were the discounts typical of the consumer goods market: 'buy two, get one free' and 'two vacuum-packed bags of ground coffee sold as one' offers are the most common.

The main competitors

In 1988 the major competitors were as follows:

Lavazza SpA of Turin Family-owned and the tenth largest food company in Italy, it was the coffee market leader and the only company to offer a complete product line. Lavazza distributed nationally eleven brands and blends at different price-points and with differences in taste and quality. Its leadership was heavily supported by advertising for every brand. In 1988 the company image was promoted through testimonial advertising showing a famous Italian actor presenting the 'Italianness' of Lavazza coffee. Television commercials also emphasized the quick stimulating effects of the coffee: 'The more you push it down, the more it pulls you up!'

Segafredo-Zanetti SpA of Bologna This company traditionally concentrated on normal roasted coffee and in moving into the family segment for the first time was among the first to introduce the combination pack of two vacuum-packed bags of coffee. Segafredo had historically focused on the CHR segment, for which it also produced industrial espresso machines sold under the name Segafredo. The company offered a wide variety of roasted blends and it invested heavily in sponsoring both national and international sporting events.

Crippa & Berger SpA of Milan This was the first company to produce decaffeinated coffee in Italy. The firm competed directly with Nestlé through its own brand of instant coffee, Faemino, but its particular strength lay in its decaffeinated coffee Hag (65% market share, versus 27% of Lavazza decaffeinated brand). Crippa & Berger's brands were:

Gah (a new product featuring low caffeine and low fat), Faemino and Hag. It invested nearly 28% of its revenue in advertising, principally to promote the brand name Hag.

Crippa & Berger advertising was mainly aimed to justify the premium price of the Hag brand, in both the CHR and family segments. It presented the several different benefits that the consumer can get from using a decaffeinated coffee, in several different contexts. The firm did not invest in supporting the instant coffee Faemino brand.

Procter & Gamble Italia The Italian subsidiary of the Cincinnati-based multinational, with its Splendid brand, benefited from strong distribution penetration due to the broad range of the group's grocery products. P&G promoted the Splendid brand by sponsoring television programmes with high viewer ratings (e.g. the most successful Italian variety show, *Fantastico*, in 1988).

The year 1988 was unusual because the advertising budget for Splendid Decaffeinato, close to $15 million, was for the first time more than what was budgeted for normal roasted coffee. The positioning was different for the different products: Splendid Oro and Classic were presented as the coffee used in the most prestigious restaurants; the other product in the line was targeted, through aggressive promotion, to the large family segment.

Illy Caffè of Trieste This firm produced one blend of normal coffee which seven different degrees of roasting. Illy Caffè was well known for its excellent quality and a series of decaffeinated and low-caffeine coffees (Mite).

All the Illy commercials tried to show that Illy espresso was better than any other coffee brand: 'the best, maestro' was the answer of an American patron to the coffee shopkeeper who asked his opinion of Illy espresso. The campaigns were briefly suspended in 1988 because of the intervention of the Italian equivalent to the United States' Federal Communication Commission (FCC) in relation to comparative advertising, strictly forbidden in Italy. Yet this did not stop the firm from improving its market position.

Consorzio Sao Café The firm licensed its brand name to eight different companies that undertook the production and distribution of the Sao brand. The advertising budget was centrally managed and represented one of the most important elements in co-ordinating the activities of the consortium. Its commercials focused on the Brazilian sound of the name, using the positive association between the country of origin ('from Brazil: Sao café') and the high coffee quality.

Café do Brasil The company had a strong brand in Caffè Kimbo, favoured especially in Southern Italy where consumers enjoyed its strong and bitter flavour. Kimbo coffee had rapidly gained in market share as a result of competitive prices coupled to a strong advertising effort. The TV commercials of Kimbo were based on a very popular testimonial personality (Pippo Baudo) tasting the strong flavour of the coffee in a roaster plant and emphasizing the consequent freshness and rich taste of Kimbo coffee.

The small coffee processors bought raw coffee from importers and sold this to different local outlets. Often these companies were able to offer a high-quality product adapted to the tastes and traditions of the regions in which they operated.

Nescafé in Italy

Instant coffee was introduced into Italy in 1962. The flavour of Nescafé in Italy was particularly 'Italian' due to the degree of roasting, the type of solubilization and the raw materials used (more Robusta and less Arabica). This always made the formulation of Nescafé in Italy something particular and different from that in the other European countries.

The Italian market possessed a very specific and deep-rooted coffee 'culture'. Nestlé's main objective when it launched Nescafé was to have the product, although soluble, perceived as 'real' coffee.

Marketing decisions were aimed at overcoming the inevitable suspicions of a coffee that was simultaneously 'good, convenient and easy to use', a phrase often voiced in Nestlé Italy's marketing office. As a result, every effort was made to affirm the goodness and quality of the product, comparing it directly to other Italian coffees.

The advertising message, essentially aimed at an emotional response, underscored the goodness of the coffee with claims such as: 'Hmm, what is it? . . . What's happening? . . . I smell coffee . . . Nescafé, the best of them all'. None the less, research showed that consumers perceived the product to be a coffee which was 'missing something' and which could not substitute for 'real' coffee. Nescafé came to be viewed as a 'back-up' product only to be used in case of an 'emergency', and best suited to singles or older people.

The decision to compare Nescafé directly to Italian espresso, shown in the advertising, did not convince consumers in terms of product quality or goodness, as a 1978 study demonstrated. Meanwhile sales had remained constant at about 400 tonnes since 1972.

From 1979 to 1983 the marketing sought to obtain a more 'personal' involvement on the part of consumers. Advertising campaigns no longer centred on the product, but rather presented 'testimonials' by real people.

The marketing department adopted a 'multi-subject' campaign which showed 'typical' people in the workforce: a forest ranger, a dockworker, a train driver, etc. The campaign aimed to show that Nescafé was coffee suited to and made for anyone who 'wants something more out of life' and 'gives something more to it'. The claim was: 'You deserve a better coffee, Nescafé'. The advertising message was reinforced with sampling and displays at the point of sale.

However, the 1981 tracking study did not indicate any image improvement. Nescafé was still an unattractive product to those who wanted 'gratification and a "recharge"' from their coffee. Sales increased very slowly (still around 500 tonnes in 1982).

Between 1984 and 1986 an advertising campaign entitled 'The train' was imported from France after its huge success in that country. It also achieved high recognition in Italy. The advertising presented an exotic train journey aimed at stimulating emotional involvement, while the 'rational' product benefits were communicated through suggestive images of locations where coffee is grown. The adverts underscored the value of a good coffee, suggesting the positive associations with Nescafé's origins without comparing it directly to typical Italian coffee.

The 1985 tracking study showed some change in the image of Nescafé as a consequence of the new advertising; the product had gained in perceived prestige and reliability. There was a corresponding increase in sales volume. In 1986 this increased to 580 tonnes, and by 1988 it reached 640 tonnes.

The most recent study report, handed out by Mr Baruffa at the meeting referred to at the start of this chapter, showed how the consumption of Nescafé was biased towards use by older people who were more sensitive to the effects of caffeine. Nescafé was preferred because of its less 'aggressive' image and for its ease of preparation during moments of relaxation.

Thus, those aged 55 and above represented about 80% of Nescafé consumers, although their per capita consumption did not exceed one cup per day. In the broader family market Nescafé was considered 'emergency provisions' by many Italian families, especially when on holiday.

Considering that instant coffee was generally retailed to the public at 60,000 lire per kilogram, against a 13,000 lire average for normal coffee, it can be said that the product was, in relative terms, prospering in a 'splendid niche'.

The price to wholesalers was 85% of the retail price, and the variable manufacturing costs amounted to 37.5% of the retail price; therefore, there was a gross operating profit equal to 47.5%. Sales and distribution costs represented 15.3%, and all of this ensured a high operating profit of about 32.3% (see Exhibit 13).

However, Nestlé Italy's management was dissatisfied with the results so far obtained, and taking account of the wide distribution of the brand, believed that more could be done. A new strategic plan had to be developed to increase sales. Manufacturing could readily increase the quality of coffee available to support an increase.

Exhibit 13 **Costs and contributions: Nescafé vs roast and ground, average 1988 (lire)**

	250 gram (R&G)	125 gram (Nescafé)	6 gram (espresso)
Suggested retailer selling price	3,250	7,500	800
Producer selling price	2,600	6,375	111
Cost of goods sold	2,157	3,160	79.7
Manufacturing	1,490	2,812	55.8
Distribution	660	550	25.9
Contribution margin	442	3,013	29.3
Sales promotion	45	374	0.25
Trade	10	250	0.25
Consumer	35	124	–
Advertising	30	426	0.5
Contribution after marketing expenses	367	2,213	19.3

Exhibit 14 *Results of the motivational study*

The following affirmations were reported with significant frequency during the course of extended interviews on the relationship between the interviewee and coffee, in particular, Nescafé.

1   'Espresso is true coffee'
2   'Nescafé isn't as strong as normal coffee'
3   'Espresso coffee is strong, flavourful and aromatic'
4   'Nescafé isn't real coffee'
5   'Nescafé is easier to handle'
6   'Nescafé is used only in *emergencies*'
7   'Nescafé is for older people'
8   'Preparing a pot of coffee is not a waste of time' (predominant response by coffee drinkers who don't drink Nescafé)
9   'Coffee is a risky product and its consumption should be reduced'[1]
10 'Coffee, tobacco and alcohol are bad for you'[1]

Certain specific results on Nescafé
- 2/3 of Nescafé drinkers prefer it during meals or in the afternoon
- the remaining 1/3 use it as a 'milk modifier' in the morning
- the different brands of Nescafé are easily distinguished
- 43% of consumers consider it 'lighter' than an espresso or 'mocha' coffee, 20% 'as much as', 37% 'don't know'
- 40% of those who 'know' the product judge it to be 'lighter' than an espresso or mocha coffee, 10% 'as much as', 50% 'don't know'

[1] Frequently heard affirmations and associations of children and young adults.

At the meeting, Mr Baruffa wanted to present some important information on the results of certain qualitative (psychological and motivational) studies and data regarding the present consumption of Nescafé.

Among these data (Exhibit 14), the most interesting findings were

Exhibit 15 *Distribution of Nescafé vs roast and ground coffee: consumption for major Italian markets*

	Population (%)	Roast & ground (%)	Nescafé % of total sales
Rome	7	9.1	4.2
Milan	4	5.7	29.5
Turin	2.5	3.1	5.1
Naples	3.2	4.2	0.9
Bologna	2.2	2.7	2.4
Florence	1.8	1.9	2.7
Palermo	1.6	1.8	0.7

Sources: ISTAT and Nestlé Italy

those measuring the 'cultural resistance' of Italians to Nescafé in terms of the reputation and use of the product.

Nescafé brand awareness was high, at 83% of the sample population (more than 3,000). However, Nescafé had been tried by only 39%. Its share of the total coffee market was 1.4%, while its market penetration (presence of at least one Nescafé package at home) was 14%. Sales were concentrated in some big cities and in the North of Italy (see Exhibit 15).

Marketing strategy options

Mr Baruffa expected to discuss four strategic options that he presented as follows:

1 To focus on the older segment, already heavy consumers of the product.
2 To broaden the use of Nescafé, as a 'milk modifier', particularly in the morning.
3 To try to position Nescafé for younger and more 'cosmopolitan' professionals, marketing Nescafé as 'the international coffee beverage'.
4 To try to penetrate the CHR segment of the market.

Mr Baruffa began the discussion by leading on the first option. He considered it the least attractive, pointing out that the limited coffee consumption by the older people would not lead to significant increase in the Nescafé sales, though the demographic trends showed that segment as more attractive in the longer term.

The marketing director, Mr Bechi, addressed the second option presented by Mr Baruffa. He believed that, as the recent research showed, 'the youngster' should be Nescafé's main target for the next five years. However, Mr Bechi was concerned about positioning of Nescafé as a milk modifier, because of the leadership by Nestlé Italy in that category with Nesquik and Orzoro. He warned the group about the high probability of a cannibalization effect and the inevitable internal conflict with the milk modifiers' product management.

In response, Mr Baruffa pointed out that younger people's appreciation of Nescafé was an opportunity to emphasize the product both as a milk modifier and as a 'new, less-caffeine-alternative coffee'.

Mr Mazzei, the chief financial officer, argued against the option for entry into the CHR segment. He felt that the trade promotion investment in that segment would need to be so high that Nescafé sales in CHR would barely pay back the initial investment needed for entry and distribution of the product. He also thought that a significant switch from espresso to Nescafé in a coffee-shop was very unlikely.

The discussion then moved on to the proposal made by Mr Giuliani, head of strategic planning, to radically modify the Nescafé positioning, marketing the coffee as an international coffee (not as an Italian coffee) to the cosmopolitan segment that mainly lives in the big Northern cities. Mr Giuliani believed that the major Nestlé food products should become standardized by the 1990s, at least in the European market.

Mr Giuliani explained that significant organizational benefits could come from this policy and that, looking at the market-place, there was a growing 'transnational consumers' segment that, travelling and living all over the world, was achieving 'universal' consumption habits.

At this point the discussion moved towards more specific evaluation of each option, aiming to define a new marketing strategy and a new marketing plan for Nescafé.

Questions for discussion/suggested tasks

1   Which of the four options outlined in the case would you adopt and why? Is there yet another, even better alternative?
2   What would be the target segment(s), proposed positioning and promotion, pricing and distribution strategies?
3   What would be the advertising copy strategy and the budget to invest on the 'relaunch' of Nescafé?

Note

1   In 1983, 1,250,000 Italian lire were equivalent to about US $800; in 1988, 1,950,000 Italian lire were equivalent to about $1,400.

5

Dulato

Reorganizing the sales force

Bernard Dubois, Joachim Malato de Sousa and Eduardo Cruz

Mr Ribeiro, marketing manager of the Dulato Company, is worried. His sales manager has just decided to resign and has persuaded a salesman to leave the company with him. Budget constraints do not allow additional recruitment, while, at the same time, Mr Ribeiro needs to allocate one salesperson to a territory previously managed by an agent whose contract has just been cancelled.

Upon reflection, Mr Ribeiro considers that the situation he is faced with provides him with a unique opportunity to rethink his sales management policy and to reorganize his sales force accordingly.

In September 1980, Mr Ribeiro, the newly appointed marketing manager of the Dulato company, a Portuguese food-processing company, was preoccupied with a serious organizational problem in the commercial area.[1]

The company sales force consisted of twenty field salespeople and two salespeople in charge of contacts with the supermarket chains, as well as an exclusive agent in charge of the Algarve area (a region situated at the extreme south of Portugal). The salespeople reported to three supervisors, who themselves reported to a national sales manager. Exhibit 1 shows the composition of the sales force as well as their territory responsibilities, while Exhibit 2 shows the corresponding organizational chart.

In fact, Mr Ribeiro was confronted with three difficulties. First, after analysing the results of the exclusive agent as well as his compensation plan (10% + 5% + 5%, 90 days), he had concluded that, even after taking into account the distribution costs supported by the agent (estimated at 3% by Mr Ribeiro), the net compensation obtained by the agent was excessive. Thus he had decided to cancel the exclusivity

Exhibit 1   *Composition of the Dulato sales force, January 1980*

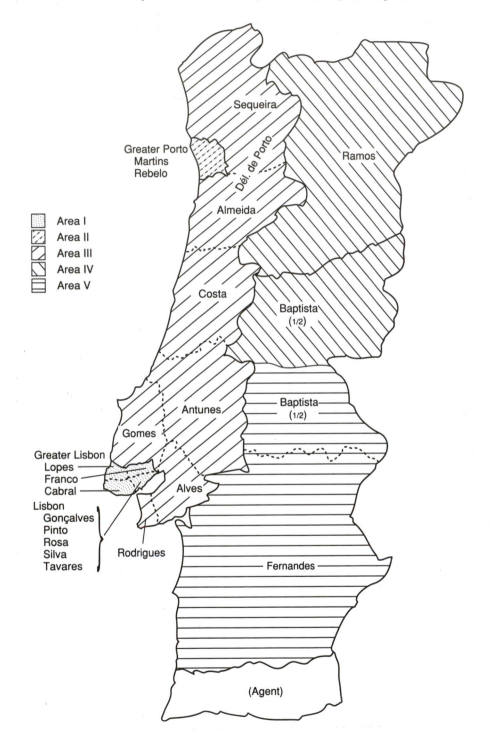

Exhibit 2   *Dulato sales department*

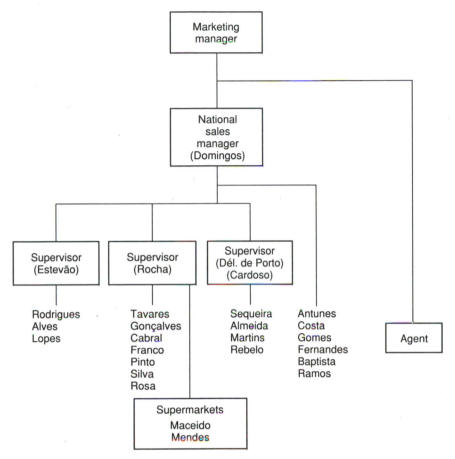

contract and to replace the agent by a salesperson. From now on, the agent would be considered as a regular wholesaler. The national sales manager who disagreed with that decision had just decided to leave the company and had convinced a salesman (Mr Gonçalves) to leave the company as well. Lastly, due to budgetary difficulties, Mr Ribeiro knew that he could not recruit any additional people. The only choice left was to reorganize the commercial department through reallocations of existing people. The problem was how best to do this.

In the Dulato company, each salesman sold the whole product line in the territory assigned to him. He received a straight salary of 12,000 Portuguese escudos[2] per month and a commission of 1% on all sales in excess of 450 contos[3] of monthly invoice. Except in the Greater Lisbon area, salesmen also received a collection premium calculated as follows: 10 escudos for each invoice less than 2,000 escudos, 15 escudos for each invoice between 2,000 and 10,000 escudos and 20 escudos for each invoice

Exhibit 3   Dulato Sales Statistics, January–June 1980

	Sales									Costs (contos)				
	Sales (contos)	No. visits	Sales/ visits	No. invoices	Conversion rate (orders/ visits)	Sales/ invoices	Fixed salary (12,000/ month)	Commis. (1% > 450/ month)	Coll./ premium	Paid holidays and 13th month (sal. + com. + prem.)	Reimb. sub-sistence	Km travelled	Total costs	Costs/ sales
Area 1														
Tavares	9,255	1,862	4.97	1,243	66.8	7.45	72	69.6	–	23.6	7.5	4.7 (F)	213.5	2.3
Goncalves	11,592	1,829	6.34	1,143	62.5	10.14	72	88.9	–	26.8	–	4.7 (F)	233.4	2.0
Cabral	11,847	2,740	4.32	1,637	59.7	7.24	72	82.7	–	25.8	19.4	86.5	325.8	2.7
Franco	9,800	2,217	4.42	1,257	56.7	7.80	72	77.6	–	24.9	17.2	77.9	307.8	3.1
Pinto	9,819	2,724	3.60	1,338	49.1	7.34	72	85.8	–	26.3	5.8	37.6	262.7	2.7
Silva	8,670	2,566	3.38	1,185	46.2	7.32	72	58.8	–	21.8	5.6	2.5 (F)	194.1	2.2
Rosa	10,519	2,022	5.20	1,091	54.0	9.64	72	73.6	–	24.3	–	4.0 (F)	211.0	2.0
Lopes	13,190	2,272	5.81	1,189	52.3	11.09	72	93.9	–	21.7	18.2	94.0	348.1	2.6
Area II														
Martins	10,288	1,268	8.11	1,040	82.0	9.89	72	62.6	4.3	23.2	–	1.6	199.8	1.9
Rebelo	14,849	1,859	7.99	1,185	63.7	12.53	72	115.2	4.1	31.9	8.8	101.2 (F)	382.0	2.6
Area III														
Sequeira	13,554	1,453	9.33	917	63.1	14.78	72	99.3	9.6	30.2	50.4	111 (I)	418.6	3.1
Almeida	12,149	1,434	8.47	937	65.3	12.97	72	89.7	11.8	28.2	50.3	124.5 (I)	421.5	3.5
Antunes	16,850	2,079	8.10	1,253	60.3	13.45	72	130.9	18.6	36.9	30.8	111.4 (F)	457.1	2.7
Costa	22,788	1,880	12.12	998	53.1	22.83	72	183.2	11.4	44.4	41.3	121.5 (I)	541.8	2.4
Gomes	9,943	1,846	5.39	671	36.3	14.82	72	81.6	7.6	26.9	34.7	104.7	368.6	3.7
Rodrigues	11,247	2,432	4.62	1,250	51.4	9.00	72	60.9	3.7	22.8	14.4	66.6	257.2	2.4
Alves	12,828	1,971	6.51	656	33.3	19.55	72	105.4	1.9	29.9	11.6	67.7	334.2	2.6

Exhibit 3 *continued*

| | Sales | | | | | | Costs (contos) | | | | | | | |
	Sales (contos)	No. visits	Sales/ visits	No. invoices	Conversion rate (orders/ visits)	Sales/ invoices	Fixed salary (12,000/ month)	Commis. (1% > 450/ month)	Coll./ premium	Paid holidays and 13th month (sal.+ com.+ prem.)	Reimb. sub-sistence	Km travelled	Total costs	Costs/ sales
Areas IV and V														
Ramos	11,083	1,161	9.55	476	41.0	23.28	72	67.2	4.5	24.0	41.2	–	245.5	2.2
Baptista	9,345	999	9.35	342	34.2	27.32	72	67.0	3.6	23.8	37.1	–	239.8	2.6
Fernandes	21,489	1,349	15.93	698	51.7	30.79	72	170.8	7.2	41.7	30.1	–	385.5	1.8
Supermarkets														
Maceido	14,338	825	17.38	865	104.8	16.58	72	58.3	–	21.7	3.4	24.5	213.1	1.5
Mendes	10,841	940	11.53	1,252	133.2	8.66	72	77.6	2.1	25.3	2.2	73.2	291.1	2.7
Agent	14,024													
Total	276,284	39,728		22,623			1,584	2,000.6	90.9	612.6	430	1,214.8	6,870.2	

(F) = fixed amount

above 10,000 escudos. In addition, they were entitled to one month of paid holiday as well as a thirteenth month. The corresponding payments were calculated on the basis of the sum: fixed salary + commission + premium. Salesmen's expenses were reimbursed on the basis of invoices for hotel and restaurant expenditures and 11.25 escudos per km in the case of travel expenditures (certain salespeople, however, received a fixed amount of 4,700 escudos). Finally, social expenses were calculated at 25.5% of the sum: salary + commission + premium. At the end of each day, every salesman had to fill out a report in which he indicated how many visits were made during the day, the number and quantities of orders, the reasons for no orders, kilometres travelled, incurred expenses, as well as other information useful for commercial planning.

Mr Ribeiro was concerned. He wanted to reorganize the sales department in a way that would be both efficient for the company and fair for the sales force. He wanted to have a selling cost percentage that would be more or less the same in all territories but, at the same time, he wanted the compensation levels to be not too dissimilar from each other, except for reflecting actual competence or performance. The workload also had to be more or less comparable from one territory to the next. Finally, he wanted all the territories to have a comparable potential so as to offer comparable opportunities for progress.

Steps towards reorganization

In order to facilitate progress towards a decision, Mr Ribeiro had prepared several documents as follows:

1   A comparative table indicating, for each salesman and for the first semester of 1980 (a period which was considered sufficiently representative by Mr Ribeiro):
    - sales;
    - number of visits;
    - average sales per visit;
    - number of orders (invoices) obtained;
    - conversion rate (orders/visit ratio);
    - average sales per order;
    - fixed salaries;
    - commissions;
    - collection premiums;
    - paid holidays and thirteenth month (on a proportional basis);
    - reimbursements for hotels and restaurants;
    - reimbursements for kilometres;
    - total costs (including social charges);
    - selling cost percentages (total costs/sales).

    This table is presented in Exhibit 3.

Exhibit 4 *Index of purchasing power, continental Portugal*

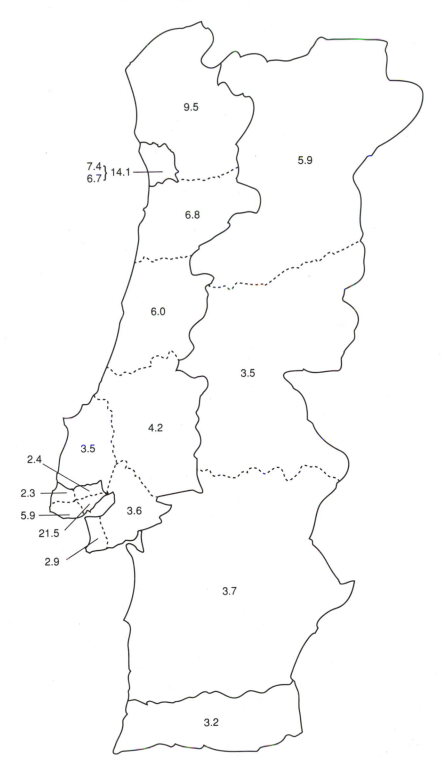

Exhibit 5   *Profile of the Dulato sales force*

Salespeople	Born in	Age in 1980	Joined the company in
Tavares	1943	37	1972
Pinto	1936	44	1971
Franco	1942	38	1971
Lopes	1943	37	1971
Maceido	1920	60	1965
Silva	1955	25	1973
Baptista	1945	35	1971
Ramos	1938	42	1972
Cabral	1930	50	1971
Mendes	1948	32	1973
Rodrigues	1927	53	1965
Antunes	1936	44	1969
Costa	1946	34	1971
Fernandes	1943	37	1972
Alves	1943	37	1972
Sequeira	1931	49	1971
Martins	1944	36	1971
Almeida	1940	40	1971
Rebelo	1940	40	1971
Gomes	1938	42	1965
Gonçalves	1947	33	1980
Rosa	1937	43	1970

2   An estimate of the potential of each territory. This was based on an index of purchasing power that was available from a market research company report that Mr Ribeiro had purchased. The index was calculated on the basis of several indicators (demographic, commercial, economic and fiscal) for each *concelho* (district) of continental Portugal. On that basis, Mr Ribeiro had calculated the potential for each sales territory (Exhibit 4).

3   A profile of each member of the sales force (age, number of years spent in the company, etc.) (Exhibit 5).

In addition, Mr Ribeiro was concerned about the commercial procedures in use in the company. Until then, no clear policy regarding sales calls had been clearly established (frequency and duration of sales calls, intensity of prospection activity). Each salesman decided, on the basis of his experience in the territory, which customers he wanted to contact as well as the rhythm of calls. Mr Ribeiro was very unhappy about this. He felt that salespeople were misallocating their efforts and were more concerned about sales than about profitability (assuming an average discount of 8.5%, the commercial net margin was about 11.7% of sales). In order to make a decision, Mr Ribeiro had prepared, for each salesperson, a listing of sales obtained in 1979 (Exhibit 6), broken down

Exhibit 6 Dulato sales by salesperson (named) and by type of customer, 1979

Categories of customers	Sequeira		Martins		Rebelo		Ramos		Baptista		Almeida	
	Sales (contos)	Customers (no.)	Sales (contos)	Customers (no.)	Sales (contos)	Customers (no.)	Sales (contos)	Customers (no.)	Sales (contos)	Customers (no.)	Sales (contos)	Customers (no.)
< 15 cts/year	1,185	158	1,500	200	1,807	241	442	59	315	42	900	120
15–30 cts	1,777	79	1,642	73	1,350	60	900	40	450	20	2,610	50
30–50 cts	2,360	59	1,880	47	1,680	42	1,560	39	520	13	1,480	37
50–100 cts	4,200	56	2,700	36	2,775	37	2,850	38	2,100	28	2,625	35
100–250 cts	6,825	39	4,025	23	3,850	22	6,300	36	2,625	15	7,000	40
250–500 cts	750	2	3,750	10	2,625	7	1,875	5	2,250	6	3,750	10
500–1,000 cts	–	–	1,500	2	1,500	2	750	1	1,500	2	750	1
> 1,000 cts	–	–	1,500	1	4,500	3	–	–	–	–	–	–
Total	17,097	393	18,497	392	20,087	414	14,677	218	9,760	126	19,115	293

Categories of customers	Antunes		Gomes		Franco		Lopes		Rosa		Pinto	
	Sales (contos)	Customers (no.)	Sales (contos)	Customers (no.)	Sales (contos)	Customers (no.)	Sales (contos)	Customers (no.)	Sales (contos)	Customers (no.)	Sales (contos)	Customers (no.)
< 15 cts/year	1,614	203	495	66	832	111	1,777	177	1,170	156	2,077	277
15–30 cts	2,992	133	967	43	1,597	71	2,610	116	3,780	116	3,037	135
30–50 cts	3,240	81	1,760	44	1,760	44	3,200	80	2,240	56	1,840	46
50–100 cts	4,050	54	2,625	35	1,950	26	3,225	43	1,650	22	2,325	31
100–250 cts	6,475	37	4,200	24	2,450	14	3,325	19	1,573	9	2,450	14
250–500 cts	6,750	18	5,625	15	2,625	7	4,500	12	1,875	5	1,875	5
500–1,000 cts	750	1	3,000	4	6,000	8	2,250	3	3,750	5	2,250	3
> 1,000 cts	1,500	1	1,500	1	3,000	2	–	–	1,500	1	1,500	1
Total	27,372	528	20,172	232	20,215	283	20,887	450	16,100	370	17,355	512

Continued

Exhibit 6 *continued*

Categories of customers	Gonçalves Sales (contos)	Customers (no.)	Tavares Sales (contos)	Customers (no.)	Maceido Sales (contos)	Customers (no.)	Mendes Sales (contos)	Customers (no.)	Cabral Sales (contos)	Customers (no.)	Rodrigues Sales (contos)	Customers (no.)
< 15 cts/year	1,912	255	1,785	238	1,005	134	37	5	1,575	210	1,057	141
15–30 cts	1,845	82	2,160	96	1,012	45	157	7	2,610	116	1,845	82
30–50 cts	1,400	35	2,640	66	800	20	160	4	2,640	66	2,560	64
50–100 cts	1,050	14	1,800	24	750	10	1,200	16	2,475	33	2,100	28
100–250 cts	3,500	20	1,750	10	1,050	6	6,650	38	1,925	11	1,575	9
250–500 cts	3,000	8	375	1	4,875	13	6,000	16	1,125	3	2,625	7
500–1,000 cts	750	1	1,500	2	4,500	6	2,250	3	2,250	3	1,500	2
> 1,000 cts	3,000	2	3,000	2	10,500	2	–	–	1,500	1	3,000	2
Total	6,457	417	15,010	439	24,492	241	16,455	89	16,100	443	16,262	335

Categories of customers	Silva Sales (contos)	Customers (no.)	Alves Sales (contos)	Customers (no.)	Costa Sales (contos)	Customers (no.)	Fernandes Sales (contos)	Customers (no.)	Total Sales (contos)	Customers (no.)
< 15 cts/year	2,145	286	412	55	690	92	172	23	24,367	3,249
15–30 cts	2,745	122	855	38	1,395	62	382	17	36,067	1,603
30–50 cts	2,600	65	1,640	41	2,040	51	1,200	30	41,200	1,030
50–100 cts	2,700	36	2,925	39	4,275	57	3,000	40	55,350	738
100–250 cts	2,100	12	3,850	22	8,575	49	4,900	28	86,975	497
250–500 cts	1,500	4	2,625	7	6,750	18	8,250	22	75,375	201
500–1,000 cts	1,500	2	3,000	4	6,000	8	5,250	7	52,500	70
> 1,000 cts	1,500	1	1,500	1	4,500	3	4,500	3	48,000	32
Total	16,790	528	16,805	207	34,225	340	27,655	170	419,835	7,420

by type of customers, with an indication of the number of customers in each segment.

Taking into account these pieces of information, Mr Ribeiro was wondering what his final decision should be.

Questions for discussion/suggested tasks

1   Was it a good idea to cancel the contract with the agent?
2   Who should be promoted to sales manager?
3   How would you reorganize the Dulato sales force?

Notes

1   The real business situation has been modified to serve the purpose of this case-study.
2   In 1981, 1 Portuguese escudo was more or less equivalent to 1 US cent.
3   1 conto = 1,000 escudos.

6

Nico Duin BV
A small company internationalizes

Ron J.H. Meyer and Ad T. Pruyn

Much of the literature and research on internationalization is focused on large companies. This bias is reflected in the educational programmes offered by business schools, the concepts that are employed and the cases that are discussed. Yet the internationalization of small companies reveals much about the fundamental motives and problems accompanying the processes of internationalization. This case explores the situation of a small Dutch company taking its first steps into the international arena. It addresses the strategic steps faced by the company as it considers how it should go about entering the German market.

As Peter Duin puts down the phone on this sunny April morning in 1991, he wonders whether the approach to the German market he has just decided upon is the best one. As head of Nico Duin BV, a small Dutch machine factory started by his father, Peter Duin has just called his forwarder to ship a number of standard machines to Germany for the Hanover Messe (trade fair). This biannual trade show for industrial machinery companies, which will be held in May, will bring together many buyers and suppliers in this industry, and could therefore be a very suitable starting-point for active penetration of the German market. More particularly, Peter Duin is hoping to make contacts with a number of German distributors, who could sell and service his machines in key regions of Germany. However, Peter Duin isn't quite sure whether exporting via distributors is the best entry mode, especially given the mixed success of using distributors in the Dutch market. Maybe, he asks himself, the use of an alternative entry strategy would make more sense.

History of the company 1955–87

After the destruction during the Second World War, a period of reconstruction took place in the Netherlands, which, together with the post-war baby boom, led to a sharp increase in the demand for housing. The consequent wave of construction, in turn, led to a substantial growth in the demand for related tools and machines. Nico Duin, a technically trained entrepreneur living in Wormerveer, just north of Amsterdam, exploited this surge in demand by founding a machinery company in 1955, specializing in equipment for the wood-processing industry. Duin's products included frame cramps, glue presses and tenoners, which could be used by carpenters, construction companies, door factories and window-frame producers – basically anyone using wood as a building material (see Exhibit 1 for a description of these machines, and Exhibits 2, 3 and 4 for illustration).

While initially a purely domestic company, after a few years Nico Duin made his first foreign sales, although they were based on unsolicited orders from abroad, by customers who had seen his products in the Netherlands. However, these export sales never amounted to more than a few per cent of turnover. Nico Duin had very little reason to internationalize, since the Dutch market was far from mature, and all the machines he produced could easily be sold domestically.

Exhibit 1   *Nico Duin's product assortment*

Nico Duin BV makes three categories of products:

1 *Frame cramps.* Frame cramps are used to hold wooden doors and window frames in the right position under the right pressure, so work can be carried out and glue can dry. The smallest machine is approximately 2 × 3 metres and can hold a frame of up to 1.5 × 2.5 metres. The biggest machines are approximately 4 × 7 metres. All cramps come in pneumatic and hydraulic versions. Prices range from about 7,000 to 20,000 guilders. Nico Duin's frame cramps are sometimes more expensive than those of the competition, but have a better price/quality ratio and are well known for their flexibility in usage. This product category represents more than 50% of Nico Duin's sales.
2 *Glue presses.* These products are related to the frame cramps, but are used to hold together large wood surfaces, such as table tops, while the glue between various layers or parts is hardening. These machines are also highly standardized, and sizes and prices are similar to those of the frame cramps. Glue presses account for approximately 30% of turnover.
3 *Tenoners.* These are actually milling-machines solely used on window frames. This relatively new addition to Nico Duin's product assortment comes in a conventional manually guided version, but also in a computer-guided version. Peter Duin is particularly proud of this CNC 900 tenoner, which he developed himself. This machine is extremely flexible; any type of window frame can be made with the same machine, and the set-up time for each new product is a fraction of that of conventional machines. The gross profit on the sale of each of these machines is quite high, but it will take a couple of years before the R&D costs are earned back.

'The focus of our export efforts is on the first two categories of machines,' states Duin, 'because I have the most experience with them and I see the fewest problems . . . they all work at the flick of a switch.' These standard products can be easily installed and serviced by a third party. As for the tenoner, however, it is still a complex specialized product, with the occasional start-up problems, so 'We'll slowly ease it into the Dutch market, while we'll be more aggressive abroad with the frame cramps and glue presses.'

Exhibit 2   *A Duin frame cramp*

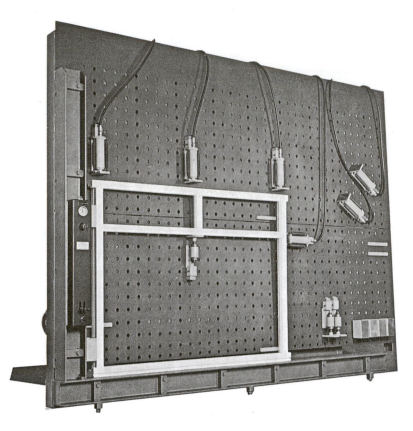

Like father, like son? (1987 to now)

In 1987 Nico Duin's only son, Peter, took over the flourishing company, but left the company's name unchanged. In contrast to his father, Peter Duin was more committed to growing and internationalizing the company, which already had an annual turnover of 1.5 million guilders.[1] He set the following objectives for his company:

1   Increase profits.
2   Consolidate market share in the Netherlands.
3   Enlarge market share outside the Netherlands.
4   Spread risk.
5   Achieve controlled growth.

Enlarging sales outside of the Netherlands was seen as particularly important, since Peter Duin expected the Dutch market, in which the

Exhibit 3   *A Duin glue press*

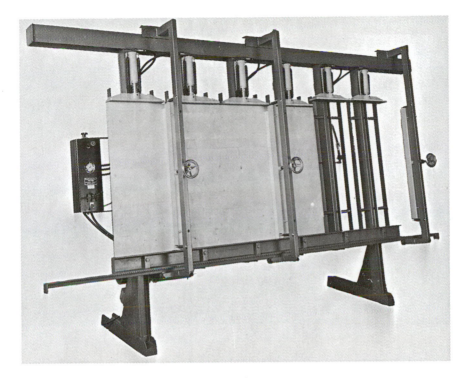

company almost had a monopoly position, to rapidly reach maturity. The installed base of machines hardly needed expansion, he believed, while the replacement market would remain small due to the high quality, and thus long life span, of the existing machinery. Sales outside of the Netherlands would also lessen the dependence on the Dutch market's building cycles. In the first instance, Duin planned to seek international expansion through exporting to surrounding countries. However, looking further into the future he did not rule out a different, more profitable entry mode.

By April 1991 Duin was able to enlarge foreign sales to approximately 15% of turnover. Most of these sales were in Britain, where Duin sold his products through a local producer of wood-working machinery, Wilson, who was focused on complementary equipment. He hoped to continue this steady growth of exports, especially by sales to the German market. Duin expected that the extra sales to Germany would allow him to increase turnover by 10–15% per year for the foreseeable future, although this would require a far more intense marketing campaign in Germany than the company's traditional 'wait-and-see' approach.

On the other hand, Duin was nervous that he might be the victim of

Exhibit 4   *A Duin tenoner*

his own success. One of the company's key objectives was 'controlled growth', and Duin was uneasy about the possibility of demand outstripping supply. He was unwilling to expand supply quickly, because rapid expansion implied borrowing money. 'I hate banks,' Duin says. 'I don't want to borrow money to bring my production capacity up to par, I want to earn it myself. I want to grow as much as possible and then stop to make some more money . . . I always have a shortage. In other words, I want controlled growth.'

Factors affecting the internationalization strategy

The production process

The production of machines at Nico Duin BV is largely a design-and-assembly operation. Most components are supplied off the shelf by other companies and are put together in a job-shop production process involving eleven people. Most standard products can be made within a week, the main constraint being the timely delivery of components. Small surges in demand can usually be met by hiring in third parties to take over some assembly tasks outside the company.

If foreign demand remains at a high level, however, Duin will be forced to increase his production capacity. From a profit perspective, making the products oneself is also more appealing than subcontracting. According to Duin: 'Subcontracting isn't the cheapest approach, but it is effective. If the stream of orders keeps coming, though, I'll expand. I'll build a second factory, or we'll take one over.'

How difficult it is to determine the optimal production capacity was illustrated during the last twelve months. In 1990 capacity usage hit 95%, which is much too high, and much production had to be contracted out. The first months of 1991 have shown a downturn, however, as the construction industry, partially influenced by the uncertainties surrounding the Gulf War, has slumped.

Research and development

Beside spending his time on general management and sales questions, Peter Duin, who like his father had a technical education, tries to invest a considerable amount of his time budget in R&D. Together with his assistant, Duin tries to translate needs conveyed to him by his customers into new or adapted products.

Duin is convinced that investments in R&D will pay off. Actually, Duin ascribes the company's current competitive advantage largely to past product innovations and the good name which this has given the company. To protect this lead the design of the CNC 900 tenoner has been patented and the software has been copyrighted. The frame cramps and glue presses cannot be protected, since their technologies are widely known.

Despite this protection, Duin has had a few cases in which his products were copied. 'Mostly these are young people or ex-employees, but all I have to do is drop my price one or two times and they leave the market.' The best protection, Duin believes, is not legal recourse but a well-known name and low production costs.

Competing in the German market

In both the Netherlands and Germany, Nico Duin's clients consist mainly of carpenters, construction companies and window-frame producers. In all three customer categories, Duin is specifically interested in the smaller companies, since they make up the majority of market demand.

As stated earlier, Duin has almost a monopoly position in the Dutch market. He is the only producer in the Netherlands and, according to his own account, he has been able to keep out foreign competitors mainly on the basis of brand recognition and a good price/quality ratio. Abroad, Duin's most formidable competitors are Hess in Germany and Ramarch in Spain. Hess, the market leader in Germany, will be a particular challenge, Duin expects, and the possibility of retaliatory measures should be reckoned with. However, this prospect does not scare Peter Duin at all. He believes that his lower labour costs and superior technology will give him a clear edge. All of Duin's products are of equal quality to those of Hess, but the German manufacturer is significantly more expensive, while Duin believes his margins are much lower. 'Hess's whole set-up is more expensive; he needs more parts than I do to make the same machine and next to that he has far too much overhead,' Duin remarks.

The changes in customer demand during the last few years in Germany are also to Duin's benefit. Due to changes in German architecture, there is a growing need for more flexible machines, which can be used to make different types of shapes. The Duin frame cramps use the so-called hole system, which is far more flexible than Hess's traditional beam system, which is more oriented towards square forms.

An additional advantage for Duin is that Dutch window frames are big, heavy and of high quality compared to surrounding countries, so that a Dutch machine easily meets foreign standards, while foreign producers find it difficult to meet Dutch norms. Not that they haven't tried. In the past Hess has attempted to penetrate the Dutch market, but he still doesn't have a foothold. According to Duin: 'His prices were much too high. He filled a Dutch showroom with machines, which cost him a lot of money, but finally the market punished him, although I admit I helped the market a little bit.' Yet Hess shouldn't be ignored. His turnover is three to four times higher than Duin's, and 'You know how German companies work. They're *gründlich*; in other words, an enormous warehouse and lab.'

Whether product adaptations are needed for the German market, time will tell, but Peter Duin isn't worried. 'We had the same problem when selling a few machines in England. The window frames needed an extra ridge and had to be stapled on the back. So you adapt, but the basic product is the same.'

Duin's distributors

When it comes to distribution, Peter Duin would like to approach the German market in the same way he does the Netherlands. The physical distribution and installation in the Netherlands are left to a forwarder, while most of the sales and after-sales service is left to distributors. Some orders for machines are taken by the company directly, without a middle man, but the large majority of sales go through a few large distributors, who have been given exclusivity within a certain geographic region. The prices of products sold directly to the customer are at the same level as the prices the distributors ask, to avoid a channel conflict. This does mean, however, that the direct sales are significantly more profitable, since Duin can pocket the distributors' margin.

Still, Peter Duin isn't enthusiastic about starting his own sales force. He sees many advantages of working through distributors. One important point is that the distributor bears the risk of non-payment. 'The distributor knows his customers' financial situation, while most customers are new to me, so I have to check them out financially if I don't want to mess up.' A second advantage is that the distributor saves Duin considerable organizational work, such as quoting prices, so that Duin's employees can spend their time on more important business.

Furthermore, distributors are better at maintaining customer relationships:

> The distributor doesn't only visit the customer to sell machines, but also to sharpen a saw. He's constantly around the customer and knows what they need and when they need it. He knows his area, does his daily rounds, hands out a brochure here and there, and can slowly soften up the customer for a sale.

Because of these benefits, Duin has given his distributors a high level of autonomy. 'In foreign markets I sell my machines to the distributors and that's that. I don't want to get involved any more. They have a sales office, they know their customers, so it's their business. I just make sure they get the machine they order from me.'

Duin does keep an eye on his distributors, however, and if they don't sell enough, he sacks them. Often this is necessary, because a distributor, once armed with the exclusive rights to a region, can 'put you in a drawer and forget about you'. Since they're often also the representative of your competitor, with whom they have a long-term relationship, they have no motivation to sell your products.

This makes for a love–hate relationship between Duin and his distributors:

> I'm a technician, not a salesman, and I can't really get along with traders. They're the smart guys in blue blazers ... I also notice that the Dutch distributor doesn't particularly like producers. Why? Because he's caught in the middle, between the customer and the producer. They know they're dependent on you. But if I keep my word there's no problem. But they also know damn well that if they try something funny, they're out. For a distributor that's not a nice position to be in.

Deciding on a market entry strategy

As Peter Duin has his machines shipped to the Hanover Messe to test the extent of customer demand and scout for possible distributors, he is still wondering whether exporting via distributors is the best approach to the German market. And if it is, how can he find good distributors, motivate them and keep an eye on them as well?

While he is not entirely sure about the answers to these questions, at least he is sure about the German market. He is willing to try and, if he fails, to try again, since a strong position in this market is essential for the long-term success of Nico Duin BV.

Questions for discussion/suggested tasks

1   Evaluate Peter Duin's motives for internationalization and his choice of Germany as the priorty export market. Are there other, more appropriate markets that Duin might enter?
2   What are the various alternative strategies open to Peter Duin to enter the German or another identified market? Which of these would be the most appropriate, why, and with what organizational implications?

Notes

This case was written with the assistance of Yeun Y. Tsai and Remy A. Kok. It is intended as a basis for class discussion, not to illustrate the effective or ineffective handling of an administrative situation. All information in the case was obtained with the kind assistance of Nico Duin BV.

1   1 guilder (abbreviation Dfl) is roughly approximate to 0.90 DM and US $0.55 (June 1993).

7

Volvo Trucks Europe
Pan-European marketing

Jean-Jacques Lambin with Tammy Bunn Hiller

In early May 1989 Ulf Selvin, vice-president of marketing, sales and service for Volvo Truck Corporation, Europe Division (VTC Europe), was deep in thought. European Community (EC) directives aimed at creating a single internal EC market by the end of 1992, were reshaping the truck market in Europe. Truck buyers' sales support and service needs and demands were changing and becoming more pan-European. Competition was growing fiercer and increasingly pan-European as well.

VTC Europe had historically operated as a multi-domestic marketer, with each national importer management team responsible for the marketing, sales and service of Volvo trucks within its country. Recently, however, programmes had been initiated at both headquarters and importer level which were aimed at moving VTC Europe towards pan-European marketing. As Mr Selvin reviewed the progress of these programmes, he deliberated over whether or not VTC Europe should attempt to become a 'Euro-marketer' and, if so, what the appropriate mix was between VTC Europe, regional and national marketing of Volvo trucks in Europe. If he and his management team decided to move VTC Europe from multi-domestic to pan-European marketing, they would have to identify the critical steps which the company would need to take in order to make such a transition successful, including the implementation implications for VTC Europe's marketing strategy, marketing organizational structure, marketing information systems and human resource development policies.

Volvo Truck Corporation (VTC) was a wholly owned subsidiary of AB Volvo (Volvo). Headquartered in Göteborg, Sweden, Volvo was the largest industrial group in the Nordic region. Established in 1927 as an automobile manufacturer, the company gradually expanded its production to include trucks, buses, an extensive range of automotive components and marine, aircraft, aerospace and industrial engines. Beginning in the late 1970s Volvo diversified into the food industry, finance, oil, fruit and chemicals in order to increase the group's opportunities for growth and profitability and to counteract economic fluctuations. Volvo's structure and organization were characterized by decentralization and delegation of responsibility. Its myriad operations were united by the shared values of quality, service, ethical performance and concern for people and the environment. The group's products were marketed around the world, with almost 90% of sales occurring outside Sweden in 1988. Volvo's sales and net income totalled Swedish kronor (SEK) 96,639 million and SEK 4,953 million, respectively, in 1988, up from 1987 levels of SEK 92,520 million and SEK 4,636 million, respectively.

The first Volvo truck was manufactured in 1928. It was an immediate success and was met with high demand. Volvo's truck production expanded rapidly in the 1930s and 1940s. The profits from truck building financed the company's total operations for most of its first twenty years. It was not until the late 1940s that Volvo's automobile production became more than marginally viable. By the late 1960s, however, this situation had reversed. Despite market leadership in Sweden and the rest of Scandinavia, Volvo's truck operations had become unprofitable due to heavy competition in new export markets, combined with problems with state-of-the-art truck models which were placing severe stresses on Volvo's design and service departments. The truck business had become a drag on the company's automobile operations. Management contemplated divesting Volvo's truck operations, but decided instead to form a separate truck division (VTC).

The creation of VTC marked the beginning of major investment in and continued expansion and profitability of Volvo's truck operations. During the 1970s and 1980s VTC replaced its entire product line with new models and intensified its marketing efforts in international markets. Between 1979 and 1986 VTC became the first truck manufacturer to win the coveted 'Truck of the Year' award three times. In 1981 VTC acquired the truck assets of the White Motor Company in the United States and formed the Volvo White Truck Corporation. In 1987 White Volvo joined with General Motors' heavy truck division to form a joint venture, the Volvo GM Heavy Truck Corporation, with Volvo as the majority shareholder with responsibility for management.

VTC's truck production grew dramatically between 1970 and 1980, from 16,300 to 30,200 trucks. By 1988 production had doubled to 60,500 units. During the 1980s VTC's share of the world market for trucks in the heavy class – gross vehicle weight (GVW) of greater than 16 tonnes – doubled to 11%, and VTC became the world's second-largest producer of heavy trucks. In both 1987 and 1988 demand for Volvo trucks exceeded VTC's production capacity.

Exhibit 1 *Sales (deliveries) of Volvo trucks by market area and size, 1987 and 1989*

Market area	Number of trucks delivered 1987	1989
Europe	29,300	31,600
North America	13,200	21,500
White Autocar/White GMC	11,100	9,800 [1]
Volvo	2,100	1,700
Latin America	3,300	3,300
Middle East	500	700
Australia	400	800
Other markets	1,000	1,600
Total	47,700	59,500
of which < 16 tonnes GVW	6,500	6,500
of which > 16 tonnes GVW	41,200	53,000

[1] Includes GM's product line.

In 1988 VTC sold (delivered) 59,500 trucks worldwide. Exhibit 1 shows the breakdown of VTC's 1987 and 1988 unit sales (deliveries) by market area. The two largest markets were Western Europe and North America, which accounted for 52% and 36% of sales, respectively. Almost 90% of unit sales were in the heavy class. VTC earned SEK 2,645 million on sales of SEK 22,762 million in 1988, which represented 34% of Volvo's 1988 operating income, up from 14% in 1986. Exhibit 2 contains graphs of VTC's sales, operating income, return on capital, and capital expenditure and development costs for the years 1984 to 1988.

VTC's organization chart is shown in Exhibit 3. Separate divisions were responsible for the manufacture and marketing of trucks in Europe, overseas, in the United States and in Brazil. Trucks were produced in ten Volvo-owned assembly plants. Of the 60,500 trucks manufactured by VTC in 1988, 20,000 were produced in the United States, 17,200 in Belgium, 14,400 in Sweden, 3,700 in Scotland, 3,200 in Brazil, 1,500 in Australia and 500 in Peru. VTC's trucks were sold through a network of 850 dealers operating with 1,200 service workshops in over 100 countries.

The product development division was responsible for the design and development of global truck concepts and components. It had development departments in Sweden, the United States, Belgium, the United Kingdom, Brazil and Australia. About 6% of turnover was invested in product development annually.

VTC Europe

VTC Europe was responsible for the production and marketing of Volvo trucks in Europe. The Western European market for heavy trucks grew

Exhibit 2   *VTC's sales, operating income, return on capital, and expenditure, 1984–8*

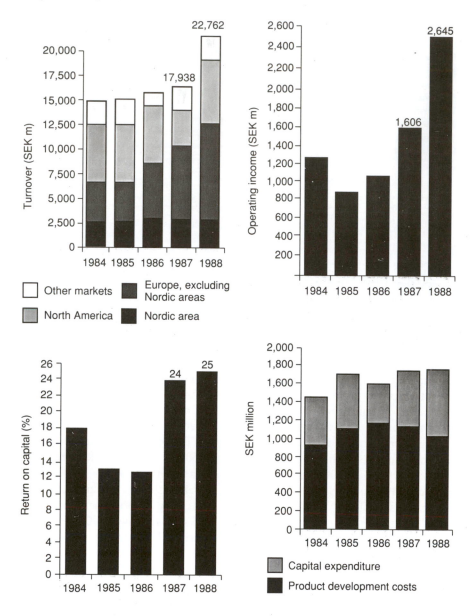

13% in 1988, to 175,000 vehicles, based on new truck registration statistics. Despite full capacity utilization of its plants, VTC Europe was unable to keep pace with the market growth. Its share of the Western European heavy truck market declined from 14.3% to 14%. The Western European medium truck market (10–16 tonnes GVW) grew by 4.5% in

Exhibit 3   *VTC's organization chart*

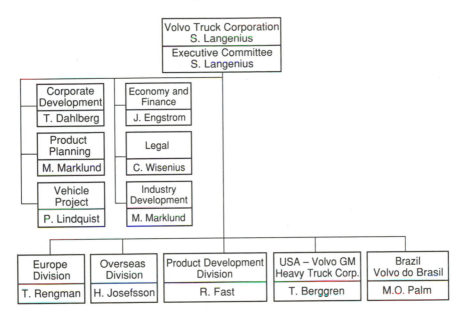

1988, to 42,000 vehicles. Volvo's share of this market declined from 10.6% to 9.0%. Exhibit 4 shows a comparison of new Volvo truck registrations and market shares by European country for 1987 and 1988.

Early 1989 registration figures indicated that Volvo was regaining lost share in Europe in both the heavy and medium truck markets, as shown in Exhibit 5. VTC Europe began 1989 with a large delivery backlog. The division dramatically improved its delivery precision between January and March 1989, moving from 56% to 80% of trucks being delivered within one week of scheduled delivery. However, delivery precision varied widely by country. As of March 1989, it ranged from 54% in Spain to 94% in Austria and Finland.

Distribution system

Two layers in the distribution system separated Volvo truck factories from Volvo truck customers. Each country's distribution network was headed by an importer that was responsible for marketing, sales and service of Volvo trucks, parts distribution and the creation and maintenance of a dealer network within its country. Of VTC Europe's fifteen importer organizations, only four – Austria, Spain, Portugal and Greece – were independent importers. The other eleven were Volvo-owned. Importers purchased trucks from VTC Europe's corporate head-quarters and sold them to the Volvo truck dealers within their countries, who in turn sold them to Volvo truck customers. VTC's European dealer

Exhibit 4   *VTC Europe sales (registrations) and market share by country, 1987 and 1988*

Market	GVW Class[2] (tonnes)	No. of new Volvo trucks registered[1]		Market shares (%)	
		1987	1988	1987	1988
Great Britain	> 10	5,720	6,610	15.5	15.4
France	> 9	4,340	4,580	10.9	10.3
Sweden	> 10	2,970	3,030	50.9	53.7
Netherlands	> 10	2,140	2,070	17.7	16.4
Italy[3]	> 9	1,490	1,780	6.5	6.8
Spain	> 10	1,010	1,700	6.5	8.4
Belgium	> 10	1,600	1,600	21.6	20.1
Portugal	> 10	1,020	1,280	29.9	27.1
Denmark	> 10	1,310	1,130	29.8	33.0
Finland	> 10	1,060	1,120	32.2	32.4
West Germany	> 10	950	1,030	3.0	3.2
Norway	> 10	1,280	800	40.6	37.5

[1] According to official registration statistics.
[2] Countries differ as to how they group their registration statistics by weight.
[3] Preliminary information.

network included approximately 400 dealers and about 800 service points. Almost all dealers were independent, although a few were Volvo-owned. All dealers were dedicated – that is, they sold only Volvo brand trucks.

The normal distribution network was rarely circumvented. Almost all sales were conducted through a dealer. VTC Europe headquarters sold directly to end customers only when selling to the governments of state-controlled countries like the Soviet Union. Similarly, importers by-passed their dealers infrequently. For example, the only customer to whom Belgium's importer made direct sales was the Belgian army

As a matter of course, importer organizations were headed and staffed by local nationals, although in a few cases a Swedish manager had headed an importer temporarily, during the transition from independent to Volvo-owned importership. Historically, importer managers were never transferred to work in the Swedish headquarters or in the importer organizations of other countries.

As one VTC Europe manager stated: 'Importers are responsible for their country – period.' Each importer's management was evaluated and rewarded on the sales volume, market share and profit earned within its country. Importers negotiated transfer prices for the trucks they purchased from VTC Europe headquarters. These transfer prices varied from country to country. Importers had the responsibility to set the prices at which they sold trucks to their dealers. Prices to dealers and, consequently, prices to truck-buying customers varied considerably by

Exhibit 5 *Total market new truck registrations and Volvo share, by country*

Market	For year ending month[1]	Total market registrations (> 16 tonnes)	Volvo market] share (> 16 tonnes) (%)	Total market registrations (10–16 tonnes)	Volvo market share (10–16 tonnes) (%)
Sweden	3/89	5,541	51.5	938	74.1
Denmark	2/89	2,317	34.7	1,379	42.6
Finland	2/89	3,827	30.3	609	34.3
Norway	3/89	1,064	45.1	203	51.9
Great Britain	2/89	39,637	19.6	5,942	8.8
Ireland	1/89	1,782	14.2	672	1.4
Germany	2/89	28,157	4.2	5,593	2.4
Europe 1	2/89[2]	83,962	18.1	14,851	14.8
France	3/89	35,921	11.3	8,371	7.3
Belgium	3/89	7,838	21.7	1,568	19.4
Luxembourg	12/88	385	31.9	86	19.8
Netherlands	1/89	9,419	16.0	1,489	22.0
Italy	2/89	27,198	7.5	13,328	2.0
Austria	2/89	3,751	14.5	1,072	7.8
Switzerland	12/88	3,349	15.4	476	19.7
Portugal	2/89	3,752	37.3	1,758	5.4
Spain	3/89	19,227	9.7	2,959	7.5
Greece	12/88	88	28.4	76	36.8
Israel	3/89	764	45.5	284	35.2
Europe II	2/89[2]	111,537	12.4	29,150	7.4
Europe total (excl. Israel)	2/89[2]	195,263	14.4	44,288	9.6

[1] The most current registration information available was used for each market.
[2] Markets with late information on registrations were estimated as of 2/89 for Europe I, Europe II and Europe total.

country, depending on local competitive pressures. For example, Belgium had no national truck producer. Consequently, the Belgian importer priced Volvo's trucks significantly higher than did the French importer, which faced fierce competition from a local manufacturer.

Marketing communications

Prior to 1987 importers had complete control of the design and execution of marketing communications programmes employed within their countries. In early 1987 Roger Johansson, marketing support manager for VTC Europe, developed a corporate communication platform. His objective was twofold. First, he hoped to encourage consistency in the visual presentation and underlying message of sales promotion and advertising materials across Europe, so as to enhance the total impact on customers of Volvo truck communications. Secondly, he aimed to improve the efficiency and cost-effectiveness of production of advertising and sales support materials. According to the communication platform, sales promotion and advertising activities were to be divided among all levels of the marketing organization – headquarters, importers and dealers – based on which level was best suited for a given activity.

The platform was designed to remain in effect through 1989. Every three years a new communication platform was to be introduced. The platform did not dictate the actual content of messages which importers and dealers could use in their communications. Instead, it encouraged creativity in designing messages which took account of local circumstances, as long as the thinking behind the messages was consistent throughout Europe. Consistency was also encouraged by a visual identity programme which strictly specified the logotypes, emblems, symbols, colours, typefaces and layouts that were authorized for use throughout the marketing organization. Responsibility for complying with the precepts of the communications platform and visual identity programme rested with the management of each importer organization.

Personal selling occurred almost solely at the dealer level. Each importer ran its own training programme for its dealer's salespeople. In addition, a state-of-the-art training facility in Göteborg was used to train both importer and dealer management whenever a new Volvo truck product was introduced. Importers and dealers were taught the features of the new truck, how those features translated into benefits for the potential buyer and how to determine the bottom-line impact which the new truck would have on the potential buyer's profit-and-loss statement.

Service

In addition to selling trucks, Volvo dealers maintained and repaired them. Each dealer was responsible for designing its local service system to suit its customers' needs. Each importer was responsible for co-ordinating service on a national level and ensuring consistency in dealer service offerings throughout its country. Volvo's service philosophy was based on the principle of preventive maintenance. Volvo dealers offered their customers service agreements with fixed prices for maintenance service and repair. Trucks that operated internationally could participate in Volvo Action Service Europe, which provided 24-hour assistance throughout Europe in the event of a breakdown. Volvo offered a DKV/ Volvo credit card to its customers, which could be used at most Volvo workshops in Western Europe and at thousands of fuel and service stations.

Volvo's service systems were not consistent across Europe. Service agreements made with a dealer in one country were not automatically valid at service centres in another country. Even when they were honoured, prices for the same service or part often differed dramatically across countries, as did parts availability. Opening hours of service centres varied within and across countries, and the work habits and quality of mechanics differed significantly from country to country. According to importer management in Belgium, few Volvo truck owners used the DKV/Volvo credit card when travelling internationally. A customer explained why: 'We do not use the DKV card any more, except for fuel. Outside Belgium, we do not have the same discount; sometimes we find a difference of up to 22% in exchange rate and sometimes the card is simply not accepted.' According to Jean de Ruyter, after-sales manager of Volvo's Belgian importer, repairs made outside of a Volvo truck owner's home country typically resulted in a communication nightmare involving discussions among the customer, the repairing dealer, the importer, the customer's local dealer and the importer in the customer's home country.

Market segmentation

Historically, VTC Europe had segmented its market solely on the basis of GVW. It divided the European truck market into three segments: heavy trucks (> 16 tonnes GVW), medium trucks 7–16 tonnes GVW) and light trucks (< 7 tonnes GVW). Volvo did not produce trucks for the light truck market. Medium-duty trucks were further split into a 10–16 tonne market, where Volvo has a large range across Europe, and a 7–10 tonne market, where Volvo sold a model on selected markets. Therefore, marketing management ignored this segment and concentrated on the other two, emphasizing the heavy truck segment in which Volvo had achieved the bulk of its success concentrating on tractors for international transport.

Marketing information systems

VTC Europe did not have a standardized method of forecasting sales across Europe. Each importer developed its annual sales forecast using its own forecasting technique. The importers' forecasts were sent to VTC Europe's marketing planning and logistics department, which used them as a starting-point for making a total forecast. Forecasts were used to plan production and for long-term capacity planning. In both 1987 and 1988 several importers underestimated annual sales by as much as 25%, leading VTC Europe to underestimate its total sales substantially.

VTC Europe's marketing planning and logistics department conducted market research and market analysis. Market research included both Europe-wide surveys and individual country surveys. Much of it was qualitative research intended to reveal how Volvo was performing relative to competitors. Results were shared with importer marketing managers. The department regularly tracked new truck registration statistics to try to discern market trends. It bought competitive production figures in order to learn the kinds of trucks which Volvo's competitors were building. The department also tracked Volvo's production, delivery precision, turnover rate and market share by country.

In addition to research conducted by headquarters, importers commissioned marketing research in their own countries as needed. Most importer-initiated market research was conducted on a project-by-project basis, rather than on a recurrent basis. There was no standardized method of gathering data across countries.

The European truck market

Between 1970 and 1988 truck sales made by Western European manufacturers grew at a compound annual rate of almost 1%. During that time, however, there were two exaggerated cycles. Sales boomed in the 1970s, peaking at 422,000 trucks (3.5 tonne GVW and larger) in 1979. In the early 1980s depression in Western Europe combined with collapse in demand from Middle East and African export markets. Sales bottomed out at 333,000 vehicles in 1984. Between 1984 and 1988 the Western European truck industry made a strong recovery. In 1988 sales reached 485,000 trucks. As Exhibit 6 shows, market growth was propelled by expansion in the heavy (> 16 tonnes GVW) and light (3.5–7.5 tonnes GVW) truck segments. Medium truck sales (7.5–16 tonnes GVW) appeared to be in long-term decline. In 1988 approximately 310,000 new trucks (3.5 tonnes GVW and larger) were registered in Western Europe.

Exhibit 6   *Western European truck manufacturers' sales by truck size, 1970–88*

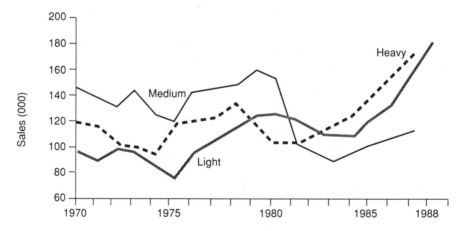

heavy = > 16 tonnes GVW; medium = 7.5–16 tonnes GVW; light = 3.5–7.5 tonnes GVW

Source: *Financial Times*, 3 May 1989

In 1950 there were 55 independent truck manufacturers, in Western Europe; in 1989 there were 11. During the 1980s several structural changes occurred in the European truck market. The most significant ones took place in the United Kingdom. Since the 1930s both Ford and General Motors had based their European truck manufacturing in the United Kingdom. In 1986 Ford entered into a strategic alliance with Iveco, the truck subsidiary of Italy's Fiat, which led to the formation of Iveco-Ford. Ford ceded management control of both its UK operations and marketing to Iveco. A few months later General Motors (Bedford-brand trucks) withdrew completely from truck manufacture in Europe after failed attempts to buy Enasa, MAN and Leyland Trucks. The state-owned Leyland Trucks was losing more than $1 million per week, when in 1987 the UK government wrote off Leyland's substantial debts in order to facilitate its merger with the Dutch truck maker DAF. DAF received 60% of the equity of the merged company and effective control. The Rover Group received the remaining 40% equity stake.

In continental Europe, structural changes were less dramatic. West Germany's Daimler-Benz, the market leader in Western Europe truck sales, reduced production capacity in the early 1980s. The other West German truck manufacturer, MAN, had been heavily reliant on Middle East markets. The 1983 cancellation of a half-completed contract with Iraq left MAN financially crippled in the early 1980s. MAN's management fought off a take-over attempt by General Motors, completely reorganized the company, concentrated on building up market presence in Western Europe and regained profitability. In 1984 Iveco closed its unprofitable Unic truck plant in France, making RVI, the truck subsidiary of Renault, the sole truck producer in France. During the 1980s RVI underwent a severe rationalization programme. By 1987 it was profitable for the first time since its formation in the mid-1970s. Enasa, Spain's only independent truck producer, entered into a joint venture with DAF for the development of a modern truck cab range which was introduced in 1987. Both of Sweden's truck manufacturers, Volvo and Saab-Scania, survived the recession in very good shape without restructuring in Europe.

There was no common classification of trucks throughout Western Europe. Although the definition of the truck market varied by country, each country maintained new truck registration statistics, which industry members used to calculate market shares. In 1988 the top five truck manufacturers accounted for almost 75% of total Western European truck sales (>3.5 tonnes GVW). Daimler-Benz (23.7%) was the market leader, followed by Iveco (20.6%), RVI (11.4%), DAF (9.4%) and Volvo (9.0%). In the two segments in which Volvo competed, heavy trucks and medium trucks (10–16 tonnes GVW only), Volvo was number two and number four in the Western European market, respectively, as shown in Exhibit 7. In 1988 the market leaders by individual country were as follows: DAF (Leyland) in the United Kingdom, Daimler-Benz in West

Exhibit 7   *Western European truck market shares by manufacturer based on new truck registrations, 1987 and 1988 (%)*

Manufacturer	Market share (>16 tonnes GVW)		Market share (10–16 tonnes GVW)	
	1987	1988	1987	1988
Volvo	14.3	14.0	10.6	9.0
Daimler-Benz	20.1	18.9	23.9	23.7
Iveco	12.8	13.6	24.9	27.6
RVI	11.9	12.3	14.3	16.3
DAF	10.8	11.6	8.0	8.7
Scania	12.4	11.0	1.3	0.8
MAN	8.5	8.3	6.2	5.0
Pegaso	4.2	4.7	1.7	0.6
ERF	1.6	2.1	–	–
WRIGT	1.7	2.0	1.0	1.0
EBRO	–	–	2.0	2.7
Other	1.7	1.5	6.1	4.6

Germany, RVI in France, Iveco in Italy, Enasa in Spain, DAF in the Netherlands, Volvo and Daimler-Benz in Belgium, and Volvo in Sweden, Denmark, Finland and Norway.

Impact of 1992 on the European truck industry

The expression '1992' was shorthand for a campaign to turn the twelve EC member countries into one barrier-free internal market by the end of 1992. The Community's goal was to create a market of 322 million people in which the free movement of goods, services, people and capital was ensured. Among the 286 legislative reforms designed to fulfil this objective were ones aimed at liberalizing road haulage in the EC. Already, transport delays at customs posts had been shortened by the 1 January 1988 introduction of a 'Single Administrative Document', which replaced the plethora of individual country documents previously required for inter-EC border crossings. Historically, inter-EC transport was strictly limited by a system of quotas which restricted the number of trips that hauliers of one country could make into other EC countries in a given year. In June 1987 the EC member nations agreed to increase these quotas by 40% per year in 1988 and 1989 and to abolish all road transport quotas to EC and non-EC destinations by 1 January 1993. As a result of these two measures, industry analysts expected a 30–50% increase in inter-EC trade by the year 2000.

The European Commission supported unrestricted *cabotage* – that is, the freedom for a trucker registered in one EC country to collect and deliver loads between two points inside a second EC country. EC member states had not reached agreement on allowing unrestricted *cabotage*, but the Commission was pushing for agreement and implementation by the end of 1992. In 1989 restrictions on *cabotage* were partially responsible for 35% of all trucks on EC roads travelling empty. Unrestricted *cabotage* would give trucks more flexibility to contract short hauls on their return trips, which would enable them to avoid returning from a long trip with an empty truck.

Trucking companies had already begun to vie for position in the EC's post-1992 transport market. Industry analysts expected concentration in the road haulage industry via mergers, acquisitions, and strategic alliances, particularly among fleets specializing in international traffic. Many observers believed that medium-sized fleets would be squeezed out in favour of small specialized hauliers and large efficient international hauliers. Most believed that the scramble for business would result in a major shake-up of the EC transport industry, after which there would probably be fewer competitors overall and, perhaps, a smaller total market for heavy trucks.

The implications for European truck manufacturers were several. Inter-European transporters had already begun to demand that truck producers supply consistent systems of service and sales support across Europe. As 1992 approached, pressures to harmonize both truck and parts prices throughout Europe would probably increase, as large fleet owners attempted to negotiate Europe-wide prices. In addition, 'artificial' differences in truck product standards – that is, unique product standards which were designed solely to protect national markets – would probably disappear over time. Eventually, new trucks might be built to 'Euro-specifications', in contrast with the existing situation in which 'every European country had two unique possessions – a national anthem and a brake system standard.' As large trucking companies became increasingly international, the loyalty of their truck buyers to locally produce vehicles would probably wane. Competition between truck producers was expected to intensify as was concentration within the industry.

VTC Europe's moves toward pan-European marketing

Market segmentation and sales forecasting

In 1984, VTC Europe took over its previously independent Belgian importer. Throughout the early 1980s, VTC had experienced heavy price competition and low profitability in Belgium. In order to develop a sound marketing strategy designed to increase the profitability of VTC's Belgian operation, while at the same time satisfying its customers, André Durieux, then marketing manager of VTC Belgium, commissioned an outside consultant, Professor Robert Peeters of the Université Catholique de Louvain, to perform a brand image study in the Belgian truck market.

Peeters designed and executed a quantitative survey of a representative sample of truck owners in Belgium.

The first objective of the study was to conceive a truck market segmentation scheme which would help Belgian management decide the right customer groups to target in order to increase the profitability of its sales. The study also aimed to discover the criteria which were determinant to truck owners when choosing a make of truck and, for each criterion, the position which Volvo and each of its competitors held in owners' minds. A third goal of the study was to determine the marketing mix through which VTC Belgium could send the right message to its target segments in the ways which would best reach them and influence them to buy Volvo trucks.

One of the outcomes of this research was the development of a truck industry segmentation scheme which Belgian management used in reshaping its marketing strategy. In 1987, Pol Jacobs, VTC Belgium's current marketing and business development manager, commissioned a follow-up study in order to assess the impact of Volvo's post-1984 marketing efforts on brand image in Belgium and to reveal any changes which had occurred in the makeup of the market by segment. Comparing the results of the second survey with those of the first showed that the pattern of Volvo's penetration of different market segments in Belgium had changed significantly between 1984 and 1987. Between 1984 and 1989, VTC Belgium improved its profitability almost tenfold. Jacobs was convinced that use of Peeters' segmentation scheme as a starting point from which to design Volvo's marketing strategy for Belgium had contributed to VTC Belgium's success.

Peeters and Jacobs had also worked together to develop an econometric forecasting model, the intent of which was to improve the accuracy of Belgium's short-term (under 2 years) sales forecasts. In 1989, the model was being tested in both Belgium and the United Kingdom. Ulf Norman, VTC Europe's manager of marketing planning and logistics, supported expanding the model's use throughout Europe if it proved successful and reliable in the United Kingdom and Belgium.

Volvo Euro truck dealer and Eurofleet task forces

In late 1988, Selvin organized the 'Volvo Euro truck dealer' (VETD) project. Its steering committee was made up of two VTC Europe headquarters service managers and five importer after-sales and service managers (from Belgium, France, Italy, the Netherlands and the United Kingdom). Chaired by John de Ruyter, the steering committee was charged with establishing the project's objectives, co-ordinating the working processes of the project among VTC, Volvo Parts Corporation (VPC), Volvo Dealer Facilities (VDF), and the importers; organizing and providing education for the importers; advising VTC and VPC in policy matters relating to the project; allocating specific tasks to work groups; and motivating all parties involved to take an active part in the project.

By the end of March 1989, the VETD steering committee had established the project's objectives and the procedures which were to be followed at importer level in order to realize those objectives. The fundamental objective of the VETD project was to create a common Volvo truck environment at all Volvo dealers in the EC (Switzerland and Austria were included in the project although they were not EC members). The desired Volvo environment was translated into specific 'Euro Dealer Standards' which applied to the external, internal, and service environments of all Volvo dealers. The importers were charged with evaluating their existing dealerships, establishing an action plan for each dealer, and following up to ensure that the plans were correctly executed.

Both the objectives and the importer working procedures were presented to VTC Europe's importer truck division managers in April 1989. Each manager was directed to appoint within their organization a VETD staff which included one specialist who would be responsible for the project. The next step would be taken in June, when the importer's newly appointed VETD specialists were scheduled to be trained.

Around the time that the VETD project was initiated, Selvin created a 'Eurofleet' task force composed of the truck division managers of each of VTC Europe's six largest importers and a headquarters liaison. The purpose of the task force was for the importers to work together to satisfy the needs of VTC's international fleet customers. Through May 1989, the Eurofleet task force had operated unsystematically, attending to each issue individually as it arose.

Pan-European management training

Selvin had identified 200 VTC importer and headquarter managers throughout Europe whom he targeted to attend a three-day training seminar at the Lovanium International Management Centre in Belgium. The purpose of the seminar was for the managers to think through, and discuss together, the changes occurring in the European truck industry due to 1992 and the impact of those changes on VTC's business. Managers were to be trained in groups of approximately 35. The groups were to be cross-sectional, made up of managers from different countries and different functional areas in order to foster the interchange of ideas and co-operation throughout the organization. The first seminar had been conducted in March 1989. The second one was scheduled for June 1989.

The future of pan-European marketing in VTC Europe

Mr Selvin strongly believed that, in order to be successfully implemented, any attempts to move VTC Europe towards pan-European marketing would require the full support of both headquarters and importer management. Importer managers would not likely support a pan-European strategy which conflicted with their local interests or was perceived as being dictated from Sweden. Therefore, Mr Selvin was convinced that it was crucial to involve managers from throughout the organization in the development and implementation of any future steps towards pan-European marketing.

Questions for discussion/suggested tasks

1 Analyse the problems and issues faced by VTC, and the strategies it might adopt, in moving from being primarily a multi-domestic marketer to becoming an effective pan-European marketer.

In doing this also consider the following:

2 How would you assess VTC's current marketing organization and competitive position? Is VTC ready for the Single European Market?
3 How might one segment the truck market, and which segment or segments are supranational segments?
4 What type of marketing organization should VTC adopt to reinforce the co-ordination of its marketing activities across Europe?

8

Procter & Gamble in Europe
A roll-out launch

Wolfgang Breuer and Richard Köhler

This case is concerned with the perennial issue for international suppliers of consumer goods – that of the relationship between global or regional approaches and those which pay attention to the particularities of local cultures and consumption patterns. For many US companies, for example, operating globally, there is the need to balance a global focus, reflecting the extent to which a great deal of product technology, research and development comes out of the USA, with a regional and/or local emphasis. Europe, comprising relatively small markets with different cultures, poses a major question about the extent to which a pan-European stance needs to be balanced with global and local approaches.

The case examines the introduction of a new haircare technology into the European market by the US manufacturer Procter & Gamble (P&G). The 'BC-18' technology enables a combination of a shampoo and conditioner in one product in such a way that the end product has the same effect as a shampoo and conditioner used separately. It had already been launched in the US haircare market in 1986 as Pert Plus, and its success was the basis for the 1988 decision to undertake a 'roll-out' launch in Europe the following year. A key issue that needed to be addressed was whether the launch of the BC-18 product into Europe should be on the basis of a pan-European brand or through adoption of more than one brand name to reflect local market needs.

Company background

Procter & Gamble was founded in the USA in 1837. Today it is the world's biggest manufacturer of packaged consumer goods and a global leader in health and beauty care products, detergents, diapers and food.

These include Pampers, Ariel, Mr Proper, Camay and others. More than one-third of P&G's total profit is generated by its international operations, which are the fastest growing part of total business. To strengthen its Health and Beauty Care Division, P&G bought in 1985 the Richardson-Vicks Company (with brands like Head & Shoulders, Vidal Sassoon, Pantene) and in 1987 the German Blendax Group (dental-care products). These acquisitions resulted in a leading position in health and beauty care products in Europe.

Over its more than 150-year history, P&G has accumulated a broad base of industry experience and business knowledge. A great deal of it has been formalized and institutionalized as management principles and policies. One of the most basic principles is that P&G's products should provide 'superior total value' and should meet 'basic consumer needs'. This has resulted in a strong commitment to research to create products that are demonstrably better than others. In contrast to the conventional product life cycle mentality, P&G believes that through continual product development brands could remain healthy and profitable in the long term.

Perhaps the most widely known of P&G's organizational characteristics is its legendary brand management system. The brand management team, a group of usually three or four people, assumes general responsibility for its brand. They plan, develop and direct their brand in its market. The group develops business objectives, strategies and marketing plans. It selects advertising copy and media, develops sales promotion activities, manages package design and product improvement projects and initiates cost savings. To carry out their responsibilities, members of the brand management team draw on the resources available to them. These include the other disciplines within and outside the organization (e.g. manufacturing, product development, market research, sales, advertising agencies). Summing up, it may be said that they know more about their product than anyone else, and they feel a real sense of ownership as they strive to develop business opportunities in their local market.

But in the beginning of the 1980s it became more and more obvious that greater co-ordination was needed between local markets in Europe. Increasingly, competitors had been able to imitate P&G's innovative products and marketing strategies, and had pre-empted them in national markets where the local subsidiary was constrained by budget or organizational limitations. Therefore, closer co-ordination was important, particularly for new brands, to ensure they reached the market-place first. Marketing strategies had to be thought through from a European perspective. This meant also the possibility of simultaneous or closely sequenced European product introductions. Furthermore, the European approach, through maximizing efficiency across countries, pooling know-how and manufacturing with better economies of scale, could give a big advantage over competition.

As a main forum for achieving this goal, the Euro-Brand Team

Meetings were introduced, chaired by the brand management of the so-called 'lead country'. This European perspective did not necessarily mean Europe-wide standardization. Market conditions still vary widely within Europe. P&G's concept is that of 'Euro-balancing', that means as much standardization as possible, as little localization as necessary. A P&G senior manager comments: 'It is occasionally better to allow some complexity to get a better overall result.'

The situation in the USA

Market development and competitive environment

The haircare market is made up of a series of sub-markets. The relevant markets for BC-18 are shampoos and conditioners. Although the constant growth of the shampoo market is mainly due to the increase in hair-washing (out of the total population, over 90% use shampoo), the growth of the conditioner market is driven by new users (see Exhibit 1).[1]

Exhibit 1   *Market sizes, shampoo/conditioner, USA, 1984–5*

	1984	1985
Shampoos		
Value (TDM)	2,400,000	2,500,000
Volume (MSU)	89,000	93,000
Use per head	375	400
(SU/1,000 of population)		
Conditioners		
Value (TDM)	1,300,000	1,350,000
Volume (MSU)	39,000	41,000
Use per head	175	180
(SU/1,000 of population)		

1 MSU = 1,000 SU (statistical units); 1 SU = 2.5 litres.
TDM = thousand deutschmarks.

The shampoo market is highly fragmented, with a large number of suppliers and brands. However, between 1985 and 1988 the relatively small market shares showed noticeable signs of movement (see Exhibit 2).

A considerable difference between the volume- and value-based market shares became visible, the cause of which lay in the relatively large price differences (see Exhibit 3).

The most important P&G shampoo brands were losing market share in the years up to 1986. Therefore, it was decided to introduce the BC-18 technology in the US market at the beginning of 1986 by replacing the brand Pert with Pert Plus.

Exhibit 2   Market shares, shampoo, key brands, USA, 1985–8 (volume (value) share in %)

	1985	1986	1987	1988
P&G brands				
Vidal Sassoon	2.5 (4.6)	2.5 (4.6)	2.0 (3.6)	2.0 (3.4)
Pert	2.5 (2.7)	2.0 (2.2)	N/A	N/A
Pert Plus	N/A	N/A	4.0 (6.0)	4.5 (6.3)
Ivory	5.5 (5.2)	4.5 (4.2)	4.0 (3.7)	3.5 (3.1)
Head & Shoulders	6.6 (12.1)	6.1 (11.1)	5.5 (9.9)	6.0 (10.1)
Competitor brands				
Suave (Helen Curtis)	11.0 (8.4)	11.5 (8.7)	11.0 (8.3)	10.8 (7.6)
Flex (Revlon)	7.5 (6.7)	8.0 (7.3)	6.8 (6.0)	5.9 (4.9)

N/A = data not available or product not on offer.

Exhibit 3   Sizes and shelf prices, shampoo, USA, 1985

	Pack size[1]	Price[2]
Vidal Sassoon	12 oz	$3.10
Pert	15 oz	$2.30
Ivory	15 oz	$2.00
Head & Shoulders	11 oz	$2.80
Suave (Helen Curtis)	16 oz	$1.70
Flex (Revlon)	15 oz	$1.90

[1] 1 oz (ounce) = 28.35 ml.
[2] In US $; 1US $ = 2.17 DM.

Introduction of the BC-18 technology in the US market

The long-term marketing goal of Pert Plus was to take over the leading value position in the US shampoo market, with a market share of at least 10% by the end of the fiscal year 1989/90. For the first year the specific target was a market share value of 5%.

In order to achieve this, Pert Plus was positioned as the shampoo that offered attractive hair in a convenient way. This was backed up by the unique Pert Plus formula, which combined a mild shampoo with a fully effective conditioner.

The target group was to be all people. The source of business would also come from the group of people who did not use Pert or a conditioner before. Pert Plus was introduced with a price of US $3.20 (for the 15 oz size).[2]

An overall summary of the basic marketing strategy for Pert Plus is shown in Exhibit 4, and an outline of the introductory activities in advertising and sales support, including timings, can be found in Exhibit 5.

Exhibit 4 *Marketing objective and marketing strategy, Pert Plus, USA*

Pert Plus marketing objective is to achieve a long-term 10% value share market leadership in the US shampoo market. Specific objective for first year of launch is a 5% value share.

1 *Positioning*: Pert Plus will provide great-looking hair in a convenient way.
2 *Target group*: all people.
3 *Source of business*: new users.
4 *Pricing*: Pert Plus will be priced within the premium-priced segment with a price premium up to 100% of the low-price market leader Suave (Helen Curtis).

Exhibit 5 *Introduction plan, Pert Plus, USA*

In the first 12 months
Ten strong TV advertising months (March–December)[1]
Household sampling (60% of households, April–August)
Listing funds ($4 million)[2]

In the following 12 months
Ten normal TV advertising months (January–May, July–November)
Sample distribution (10% of households)
Display activities in hypermarkets

Number of households in the USA: 100 millions
Start of delivery to trade: January 1986

[1] Strong advertising month means that the frequency (number of spots) is about one-third higher than in a normal advertising month.
[2] Funds paid by consumer goods manufacturer to the trade in order to place a specific product on the order list of e.g. a supermarket chain.

The development of Pert Plus's market share from the introductory year up to 1988 was shown in Exhibit 2.

The situation in Europe in 1988

Market development and competitive environment

In Europe a steady growth of the shampoo market and the conditioner market could also be seen. There was evidence of increased hair-washing. However, the conditioner market was still, compared with the USA, relatively undeveloped. The share of shampoo users who also used conditioner was still below the 44% which had been reached in the USA. This was particularly true for Southern European countries. Therefore, the initial focus was upon West Germany, Great Britain, France, Scandinavia and Benelux. An underdeveloped conditioner market was, however, also evident in France (in terms of sales volume only 10% of shampoo consumption). Among the considered European countries, Great Britain, with 42%, showed the strongest user share (see Exhibit 6).

Exhibit 6   *Market sizes, shampoo/conditioner, Europe, 1988*

	West Germany	Great Britain	France	Scandinavia	Benelux
Shampoos					
Value (TDM)	650,000	485,000	700,000	250,000	200,000
Volume (MSU)	20,000	18,000	20,000	7,000	7,500
Use per head (SU/1,000 of population)	325	325	350	300	300
Conditioners					
Value (TDM)	230,000	250,000	100,000	85,000	60,000
Volume (MSU)	4,500	7,500	2,000	1,700	1,500
Use per head (SU/1,000 of population)	70	140	35	70	70

Exhibit 7   *Market shares, shampoo, key brands, Europe, 1988 (volume (value) share in %)*

	West Germany	Great Britain	France	Scandinavia	Benelux
P&G brands					
Vidal Sassoon	0.5 (1.3)	1.1 (3.6)	N/A	1.0 (2.4)	N/A
Pantene	N/A	N/A	1.0 (2.1)	N/A	N/A
Petrole Hahn	N/A	N/A	3.0 (2.1)	N/A	0.6 (0.6)
Shamtu	11.0 (6.3)	N/A	N/A	N/A	N/A
Head & Shoulders	1.1 (1.7)	6.5 (12.0)	1.1 (1.6)	1.0 (1.4)	2.9 (5.4)
Competitor brands					
Timotei (Unilever)	5.0 (5.7)	8.5 (11.8)	4.9 (5.2)	7.5 (7.8)	3.8 (5.3)
Nivea (Beiersdorf)	9.0 (9.2)	N/A	N/A	2.5 (2.3)	4.4 (5.5)
Schauma (Schwarzkopf)	21.0 (10.0)	N/A	N/A	N/A	7.0 (4.1)
Palmolive (Colgate)	N/A	4.6 (2.7)	12.3 (5.4)	7.0 (3.0)	18.2 (10.6)
Elsève/El'Vital (L'Oréal)	3.3 (4.6)	N/A	4.5 (5.8)	6.5 (8.2)	5.0 (8.4)

N/A = product not on offer in this country.

With respect to the number of suppliers and brands, the European market was even more crowded than the US market, undoubtedly a function of the different nationalities. The most important competitors for P&G were Unilever, Colgate and L'Oréal. Some brands could be found in all countries, others only in their domestic markets (see Exhibit 7).

The gap between the top and bottom price classes was even bigger than in the US market. Between brands there were price differences of over five times for the same quantity, which meant that the value-based market share of a shampoo brand was very important (see Exhibit 8).

Exhibit 8   Sizes and shelf prices, shampoo, Europe, 1988 (DM)

	West Germany	Great Britain	France	Scandinavia	Benelux
P&G brands					
Vidal Sassoon (200 ml)	6.99	6.99	N/A	6.99	N/A
Pantene (200 ml)	N/A	N/A	4.99	N/A	N/A
Petrole Hahn (300 ml)	N/A	N/A	2.99	N/A	2.99
Shamtu (400 ml)	2.99	N/A	N/A	N/A	N/A
Head & Shoulders (300 ml)	5.99	5.99	5.99	5.99	5.99
Competitor brands					
Timotei (Unilever) (200 ml)	2.99	2.99	2.99	2.99	2.99
Nivea (Beiersdorf) (300 ml)	3.99	N/A	N/A	3.99	3.99
Schauma (Schwarzkopf) (400 ml)	2.49	N/A	N/A	N/A	2.49
Palmolive (Colgate) (400 ml)	N/A	2.49	2.49	2.49	2.49
Elsève/El'Vital (L'Oréal) (250 ml)	4.49	N/A	4.49	4.49	4.49

To simplify matters, the retail prices have been rounded off to a European average. However, price relations within a country have been retained.

N/A = product not on offer in this country.

Exhibit 9 *Media spendings, shampoo, Europe, 1988 (TDM)*

	West Germany	Great Britain	France	Scandinavia	Benelux
P&G brands					
Vidal Sassoon	1,000	3,000	N/A	1,000	N/A
Pantene	N/A	N/A	0	N/A	N/A
Petrole Hahn	N/A	N/A	3,000	N/A	0
Shamtu	4,000	N/A	N/A	N/A	N/A
Head & Shoulders	3,000	3,000	2,000	800	2,800
Competitor brands					
Timotei (Unilever)	6,500	6,500	3,000	3,000	1,500
Nivea (Beiersdorf)	8,000	N/A	N/A	2,000	1,000
Schauma (Schwarzkopf)	10,500	N/A	N/A	N/A	N/A
Palmolive (Colgate)	N/A	4,000	4,000	1,000	1,000
Elsève/El'Vital (L'Oréal)	5,000	N/A	7,000	2,000	2,000
Total	80,000	80,000	60,000	60,000	50,000

N/A = product not on offer in this country.

In order to carry through the brand message, media support was a key driving force (see Exhibit 9 and, for types of media, Exhibit 13 below).

Market research data — consumer tests

In 1988, following the success of Pert Plus in the US market, it was decided to introduce BC-18 into the European market. Key elements of a marketing strategy have already been shown with Pert Plus (see Exhibit 4). It was clear that the easy, time-saving, everyday use of the product was essential when considering positioning. There was also no doubt about placing the new product in the premium-priced segment. As with Pert Plus, a premium price was necessary to be consistent with the high-quality product concept. The main question was still, however, under what brand name to introduce the product in the individual European markets. There was also the question of whether a 200 ml bottle, used in the USA, would be accepted by the European consumer and the question of price sensitivity at premium pricing.

It was decided, therefore, to undertake some consumer research. Obviously, it was impossible to test all possible product concepts with respect to brand names, positioning alternatives, pack sizes, pack designs and price alternatives, and that for all European countries. So, in a pre-screening phase, the possible brand alternatives were reduced to four. In any case, there was to be a brand which, already present in the US and several European markets, had so far shown a certain European potential (Vidal Sassoon). The US brand Pert Plus, unknown in the European market, was also to be tested. The two other alternatives were national brands firmly established in their domestic market (Pantene and Shamtu). Price and packaging alternatives were tested on only two brands: one brand from the lower price segment and another brand which had a high-quality product concept, i.e. product concepts where possible price sensitivity would be easily detected. An abridged version of the positioning statements can be found in Exhibit 10. The consumer tests were carried out in the relevant European countries (for average results, see Exhibit 11; there were no significant differences between countries).

Economics

The criterion for cost planning for the BC-18 introduction in individual European countries was the cost structure of the existing P&G shampoo brands. This also gave an idea of the profitability of the brands tested in the consumer test, which might be one of the deciding factors in the choice of an introductory brand name for BC-18 (see Exhibit 12).

The costs of producing the new product, including average transport costs, were relatively easy to estimate, since the decision had been made to locate production for the whole European market in England. However, it had still not been decided whether to use the available 200 ml bottle or a 250 ml bottle still in development. Two figures were

Exhibit 10　*Consumer test, Europe*

Positioning statement	Price/pack size
Vidal Sassoon Wash & Go – 'for great looking hair in a convenient way'	4.99 DM/200 ml
Shamtu 2 in 1 – 'shampoo and conditioner in one – silkiness and bounce in one step'	4.99 DM/200 ml
Shamtu 2 in 1 – 'shampoo and conditioner in one – silkiness and bounce in one step'	4.99 DM/250 ml
Pantene – 'shampoo with built-in vitamin conditioner – the perfect hair care in one step'	4.99 DM/200 ml
Pantene – 'shampoo with built-in vitamin conditioner – the perfect hair care in one step'	5.99 DM/200 ml
Pert Plus Wash & Go – 'for great looking hair in a convenient way'	4.99 DM/200 ml

therefore used in the plans: production costs would be roughly 22 DM/SU^3 for the small bottle and 20 DM/SU for the larger bottle. These figures presumed a work capacity of 50%, and it was assumed that working at higher capacity would not generate lower costs because of the special production technology. To determine total costs it was necessary to consider also advertising and sales support budgets, which depended on the individual countries and their chosen introduction programme (see Exhibit 13).

Restrictions

The first restrictions arose in the available production capacity. For the first year a capacity of 2,000 MSU was available. This could have been increased to 4,000 MSU in the second year and to 8,000 in the third year. Nevertheless, in the case of difficulties, with six months' notice it would have been possible to get an extra 500 MSU capacity, but with 2 DM/SU higher production costs.

Lead times for alternative pack sizes and designs were also a restriction. The development of a new 200 ml bottle would take a lead time of twelve months. Although development of a new bottle containing 250 ml was under way, it would still take six months before it could be used. By contrast, using the existing US bottle for Pert Plus would not require any lead time.

Exhibit 11 Consumer test, Europe, results (%)

Product concepts	Vidal Sassoon Wash & Go	Shamtu 2 in 1 'silkiness and bounce'		Pantene 'perfect care'		Pert Plus Wash & Go
	4.99DM/200ml	4.99DM/200ml	4.99DM/250ml	4.99DM/200ml	5.99DM/200ml	4.99DM/200ml
'Would definitely buy'	29	20	27	28	17	28
'Is very new'	41	40	41	39	40	40
'Is very convincing and relevant'	70	73	72	73	72	70

Exhibit 12 Overview, economics/profits, Europe, 1988

	West Germany		Great Britain	France	Scandinavia	Benelux
	Vidal Sassoon 200 ml	Shamtu 400 ml	Vidal Sassoon 200 ml	Pantene 200 ml	Vidal Sassoon 200 ml	Head & Shoulders 300 ml
Volume (MSU)	100	2,000	300	200	100	400
Shelf price (DM/pack)	6.99	2.99	6.99	4.99	6.99	5.99
Manufacturer's list price (DM/pack)	4.50	2.40	4.50	3.20	4.50	4.80
Manufacturer's list price (DM/SU)	56.25	15.00	56.25	40.00	56.25	40.00
Discount (DM/SU)	5.60	1.50	5.60	4.00	5.60	4.00
Manufacturer's net price (DM/SU)	50.65	13.50	50.65	36.00	50.65	36.00
Production costs (incl. transport) (DM/SU)	30.00	8.00	28.00	22.00	30.00	18.00
Overheads (sales, R&D, etc.) (DM/SU)	5.60	1.50	5.60	5.00	5.60	4.00
Advertising costs for trade (DM/SU)	2.80	0.75	2.80	2.00	2.80	2.00
Budget for advertising and sales promotion (DM/SU)	20.00	2.50	14.00	6.00	14.00	10.00
Profit (DM/SU)	*-7.75*	*0.75*	*-0.25*	*1.00*	*-1.75*	*2.00*

Exhibit 13 Media and promotion costs

	West Germany	Great Britain	France	Scandinavia[2]	Benelux
Media (TDM per month)[1]					
TV normal advertising month	600	600	600	–	200
strong advertising month	800	800	800	–	250
Radio normal advertising month	400	400	400	–	130
strong advertising month	500	500	500	–	160
Print normal 3-month campaign	3,000	3,000	3,000	1,000	1,000
strong 3-month campaign	5,000	5,000	5,000	1,600	1,600
Sample distribution (DM per piece)					
Sample costs	0.40		As for West Germany		
Distribution costs					
Door-to-door	0.10				
Hypermarkets	0.20				
Via other products	0.15				
Additional promotions (TDM)					
Hypermarket – display activities	500	600	500	200	200
Consumer competition	100	100	100	50	50
Wheel of Fortune competition	300	300	300	100	100
Additional costs (TDM)					
Production					
TV	400	400	400	–	400
Radio	30	30	30	–	30
Print	50	50	50	50	50
Listing funds	1,000	1,000	1,000	400	300
Material for sales representatives	50	50	50	20	20
Number of households (millions)	26	22	21	10	10

[1] See Exhibit 5, note 1.
[2] TV and radio advertising not possible for legal reasons.

Questions for discussion/suggested tasks

In the light of the above, participants are asked to formulate a strategy for the introduction of the BC-18 technology in Europe, with plans for the first year of launch. In doing this, specific questions that might be addressed by participants are:

1   What are the main issues to be considered in balancing a pan-European introduction strategy with local market needs?
    • For example, what are the possible alternative brand name strategies? Should the BC-18 technology be introduced with a pan-European name, or with local brand names, or even with a mixture of both approaches? Should a new brand be created, or should an existing brand be relaunched in a new quality? What are possible criteria for that decision?
    • What is the longer-term marketing objective?
    • What are the alternative possibilities in relation to issues of positioning, target groups, sources of business, pricing strategy and packaging?
2   How would you specify the first-year marketing objective? How does this relate to the longer-term marketing objective?
3   Would you undertake a 'roll-out' launch, and if so in what country order? What are the decision criteria for this order? In answering this question you should take into account the expected sales volumes as well as the given capacity restrictions.
4   Taking the country with the highest priority, which principles would you use in order to budget media spending? Set out a rough media plan for the first twelve months, with proposals for promotion activities in the first year. How should media and promotion activities be budgeted for the following years?
5   Examine the cost and revenue implications of the Europe-wide introduction programme. Is there any loss to be expected in the first years? Does this require a modification of the order of local market entries?

Notes

The case was devised together with the German P&G office. It is based on real facts, but the figures have been partly changed for teaching purposes. A special thank-you to Dr K.P. Meier, Category Manager Hair & Skin Care Germany, for his co-operation and support in the work on this project.

1   All exhibits in this case are based on P&G sources.
2   1 US $ = 2.17 DM; 15 oz (ounces) = 425 ml.
3   Statistical unit; 1 SU = 2.5 litres; 1,000 SU = 1 MSU.

9

Export Advertising Strategies
Country-of-origin effects

Helmut J. Kurz

This case is concerned with the creation of an advertising strategy for a domestic product to be marketed internationally utilizing 'country-of-origin' effects in the advertising campaign. Participants are asked to select an Austrian product with which they are familiar and, drawing on the material supplied in the case, to develop a strategy for advertising this product in their own country.

Background: problems in today's marketing and advertising environment

Marketers in the Western industrialized countries are increasingly faced with severe problems in predicting and ensuring the success or failure of marketing and advertising strategies. These problems include the following.

Consumer 'information overload'

The consumer is confronted with an ever-increasing number of advertising appeals (advertisements in newspapers and magazines, TV and radio commercials, direct mailings). This can lead to reduced attention to advertising messages. Empirical findings have shown, for example, that the average viewing time of magazine ads has decreased to approximately three seconds (e.g. Kroeber-Riel, 1992: 72), as consumers look quickly at the pictures, the headlines and the brand name or logo to find out whether the message is useful or useless to them. Studies of TV viewing behaviour also demonstrate that more and more viewers practise so-called 'channel surfing' to identify interesting programmes, and TV commercials are often skipped using the remote control device (Opaschowski, 1992).

An increasing number of brands with similar product attributes and similar design

Many product categories are characterized by a large number of different brands and models. For example, since the introduction of the digital disc player (CD player) in 1983 the number of different brands and models has multiplied: in 1993 the consumers could select from among 250 different models. Sony even offers about twenty different models to the potential buyer. Yet the product attributes of CD players, especially the quality of sound, are perceived as very similar by many consumers. Even the design (e.g. shape, colour) of different brands of CD players is similar. The same is true for many product categories: beverages, beer, wine, cigarettes, coffee, and so on. Blind testing of brands in these product categories often shows that the average consumer cannot tell the difference between the otherwise most and least preferred brands.

Saturation of markets

Many markets in the field of consumer goods are product-saturated (e.g. Jones, 1992: 23). Marketing in such markets has become a 'zero-sum game' (what one company gains in market share, the competing companies lose).

'Emotional' advertising

Development of emotional advertising strategies

In this context, advertisers often seek to create emotional advertising strategies based on emotional appeals rather than simply 'rational' product-based attributes, as a way of differentiating their brand and developing a distinctive brand identity. A classic example of this kind of strategy is the Marlboro campaign. Philip Morris has used the cowboy motif as a symbol for freedom and masculinity since 1953. Before that time Marlboro was a cigarette for ladies.

Emotional advertising utilizing country image

Some advertising campaigns create the emotional appeal by referring to the *country of origin* of the advertised brand, using pictures and symbols typical of that country (historical landmarks, buildings, traditions, well-known public figures, and so on). For example, Pepsi used the world-famous US pop star Michael Jackson as a testimonial and the slogan 'Pepsi is New York' for an international campaign; Rolex, a Swiss watch manufacturer, showed the well-known Matterhorn in some ads; some French companies use the Eiffel tower or some 'bistro' motifs to advertise their products (for instance, wine, cheese or perfume).

Empirical studies (for instance, Han and Terpstra, 1988; Tse and

Gorn, 1993) give support to the hypothesis that consumers often use country of origin as a referent to a brand's quality, particularly when product familiarity is low (for instance, a car 'made in Germany' versus a car 'made in South Korea').

The image of Austria

To discover the key elements and dimensions of Austria's image, the Department of Advertising and Marketing Research at the Wirtschaftsuniversität Wien has been conducting surveys in about thirty countries all over the world since 1984 (see Exhibit 1 for some details of research conducted in various European countries).

The main characteristics of these surveys have been as follows.

First, for comparison purposes, images of West German and Switzerland were included with Austria in the image measurement studies. Germany and Switzerland have similar cultural backgrounds to Austria, and their inhabitants also speak German.

Secondly, verbal statements (for instance, 'beautiful landscape') as well as pictures (for instance, a picture of a scenic landscape) were presented to the respondents to represent features of the country images of Austria, Germany and Switzerland. The respondents were asked the following question by the interviewer: 'I'll read to you some statements describing characteristics of countries and people [for pictures: 'I'll show you some pictures . . .']. Please tell me for each statement [picture], to which of the following countries: Austria, West Germany and Switzerland, does it apply?' Respondents could name one, two, all three or none of the three countries. Some of the pictures used in the survey are shown in Exhibit 2.

Thirdly, the sample consisted of people with relatively high education and professional-level occupations.

The main results of these surveys – concerning the image of Austria in the European countries France, West Germany, Great Britain, Italy, the Netherlands, Spain, Sweden and Switzerland only – are shown in Appendix 1. (The results for all of the investigated countries are reported in Schweiger, 1992.)

Export advertising campaigns typical of Austria: some examples

Following the research described above, the Department of Advertising and Marketing Research at the Wirtschaftsuniversität Wien developed some advertisements typical of Austria for several Austrian products using Austrian country-image dimensions, and tested these advertisements in important export markets.

The following main advantages of advertisements typical of Austria were anticipated:

Exhibit 1 *The image of Austria abroad: surveyed countries, year of survey and number of respondents*

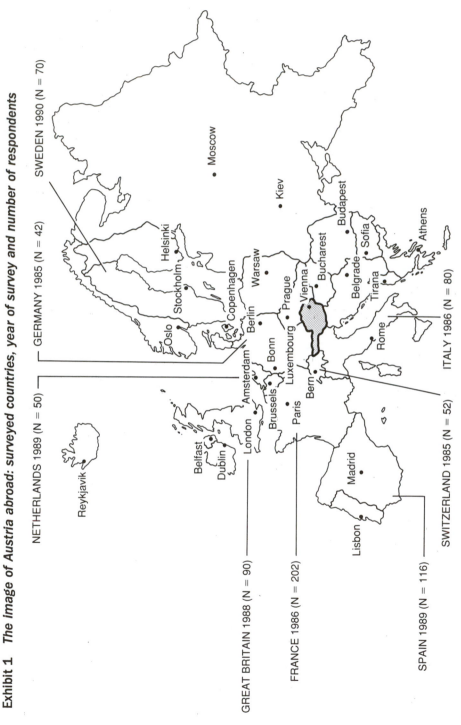

Exhibit 2 *Pictures used in the survey to measure the images of Austria, Germany and Switzerland*

orchestra

opera ball

theatre box

museum

coffee-house

buffet

Exhibit 2   *continued*

mountain peak

smokestack

skiers

vintage

UNO-city, the UN building in Vienna

- that a 'country identity' for Austria can be established just as by the Swiss, who advertise key products in foreign markets (for instance, chocolate, cheese, watches) using recognizable national symbols;
- that a so-called 'image transfer' from Austria's country image to its products could take place; for example, the precision communicated by the picture of an orchestra could be 'transferred' to a technical product by the viewer of such an ad;
- that advertisements typical of Austria would have a strong emotional appeal and therefore high effectiveness in terms of attention or brand preference by the target groups;
- therefore that the efficiency and effectiveness of export advertising campaigns run by relatively small Austrian companies can be enhanced, involving greater impact at less cost of repeated exposures, through the use of readily identifiable and memorable country-image elements.

The illustrations show three examples of advertisements typical of Austria which have been tested successfully in foreign markets.

For instance, in a test market experiment in Denver, Colorado, Schlumberger sparkling wine was ordered significantly more often by US consumers when advertised in connection with the 'Viennese way of life' than when advertised with a sales folder which showed the production process of sparkling wine according to the champagne method.

Consumer research in West Germany indicated that the ad for Schneiders fashion with the Viennese Musikverein concert hall in the background was recalled better by German women than its counterpart, an ad which showed the model in front of a wall carpet. The coat advertised with the concert-hall motif was also associated more strongly with 'elegance' than in the other version.

The ad for AKG microphones showing a portrait of Mozart and using the slogan 'Rock me, Amadeus' was tested with visitors to the world's most important music fair in Los Angeles, California. It was recalled and evaluated better by US musicians than its neutral counterpart which showed a saxophone as a background picture.

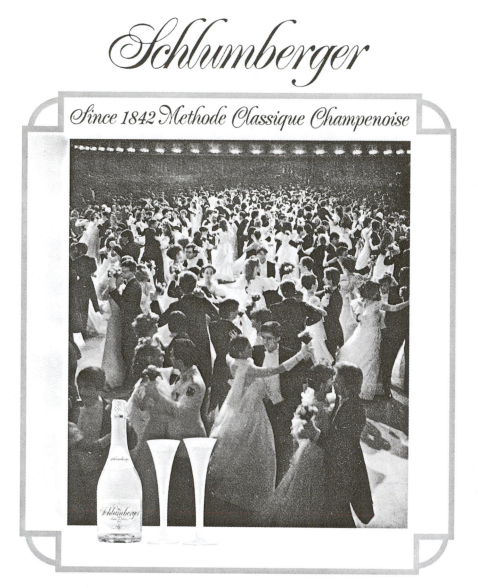

Schlumberger

Since 1842 Methode Classique Champenoise

Enjoy a Sparkling Evening as at the "Viennese Opera Ball"

ROCK ME, AMADEUS

Photo: OFW – Barti

The music of Wolfgang Amadeus Mozart will last forever. Today's technological standard has brought it from the opera house or concert hall to a great many households. Compact Disc equipment allows brilliant sound quality for everyone and forever. But even the best CD cannot make up for bad recording quality.

So if you want to preserve your music for future generations original just like used to be, excellent equipment is a must.

AKG C 525 S, is the microphone for professionals.

Sound: Absolutely natural, distortion free sound. Designed for lead vocals as well as backing choirs. For all those aiming at a professional stage show.

Design: Condenser stage vocal microphone. Operates on battery and phantom power. 1.5-V AA size battery life 300 days minimum. Frequency range 80 – 20.000 Hz. Hypercardioid polar response.

Construction: Built to withstand abusive handling on stage. Stainless steel mesh grille. Feels right in your hand and next to your lips. A microphone for sound pros and pro sound.

By the way: Did you know that both AKG and Mozart are Austrians?
For further information please write to:

AKG ACOUSTICS, INC.
77 Selleck Street,
Stamford, CT 06902/USA
Tel: (203) 3482121,
Tx. 285481 akgusa,
Fax: (203) 324 1942

Questions for discussion/suggested tasks

In the light of the above, participants are asked to design an advertising strategy for an Austrian product which involves the use of country-of-origin effects in the advertising campaign. In doing so, you should:

1 Analyse the survey data about Austria's image shown in Appendix 1 and identify the key dimensions of Austria's country-image strengths and weaknesses compared to Germany and Switzerland.

2 Choose a typical Austrian export product you already have purchased or know personally. To facilitate your research, refer to the following list of selected Austrian products and brands:

Products	Brands
Skis and ski boots	Atomic, Blizzard, Fischer, Kästle
Traditional costumes, clothes	
Microphones, headphones	AKG
Sparkling wine	Schlumberger
Cheese	
Wine	
Chocolate, sweets	

Then develop an advertising strategy for the selected product or brand and for your home country as export market. This should include:

- Define a reasonable advertising objective for the campaign.
- Set a reasonable advertising budget.
- Define a target group using demographic and/or psychographic characteristics.
- Develop layouts, roughs or drafts for ads, radio commercials, sales folders, and so on, implementing appropriate elements of Austria's image (examples are included in Appendix C).
- Develop a media strategy: which basic media (newspapers, magazines, radio and TV stations, billboards, and so on) should be used to communicate the campaign? What proportions of the advertising budget would you allocate to the media chosen?

3 In addition you should also consider the following broader questions:

- Can 'country-of-origin'-based advertising strategies be used globally, or do they need to be adapted to the particular characteristics and cultures of the different national target markets?
- What impact are country stereotypes (e.g. German cars, French fashion, Italian wine) likely to have on the purchase decisions of consumers in a changing Europe?

References

Han, Min C. and Terpstra, Vern (1988) Country-of-origin effects for uni-national and bi-national products', *Journal of International Business Studies*, 19, summer: 235–55.

Jones, John Philip (1992) *How Much Is Enough?: Getting the Most from your Advertising Dollar*. New York: Lexington Books.

Kroeber-Riel, Werner (1992) *Konsumentenverhalten*, 5th edition. Munich: Verlag Vahlen.

Opaschowski, Horst (1992) Survey for the BAT-Freizeitforschungsinstitut, Hamburg, August; 53% of the 2,000 West German respondents reported that they usually switch the TV channel when the programme is interrupted by commercials.

Schweiger, Günter (1992) *Österreichs Image in der Welt: Ein Vergleich mit Deutschland und der Schweiz*. Vienna: Service Fachverlag.

Tse, David K. and Gorn, Gerald J. (1993) 'An experiment on the salience of country-of-origin in the era of global brands', *Journal of International Marketing*, 1: 57–76.

Appendix 1: Major dimensions of Austria's image abroad

How to interpret the figures   On the left side are listed eight European countries (Sweden to West Germany) where the survey was conducted. The bars show the percentage of respondents assigning the picture or the verbal item listed in the headline to Austria, Germany and Switzerland. Respondents could assign the stimuli to one, two or all three countries or to none of them. So the percentages don't have to total 100%. Pictures referred to in the headings are shown in Exhibit 2.

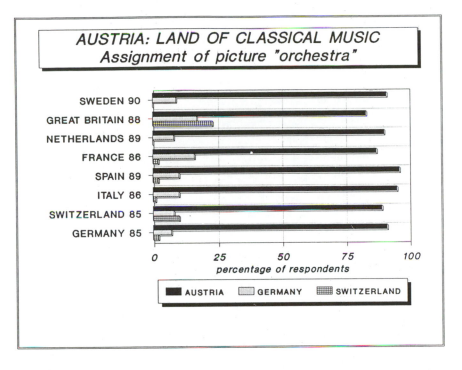

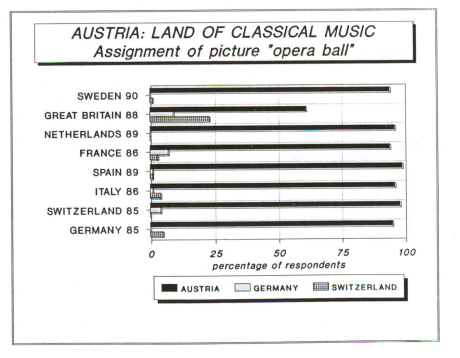

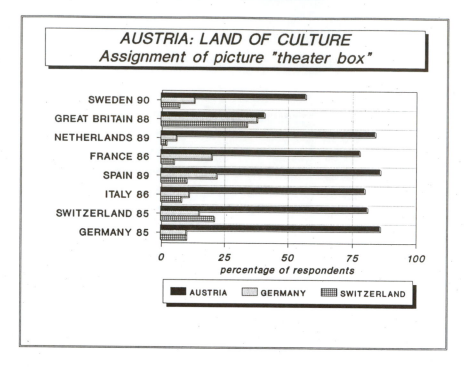

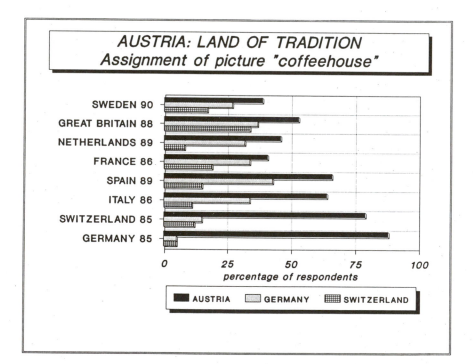

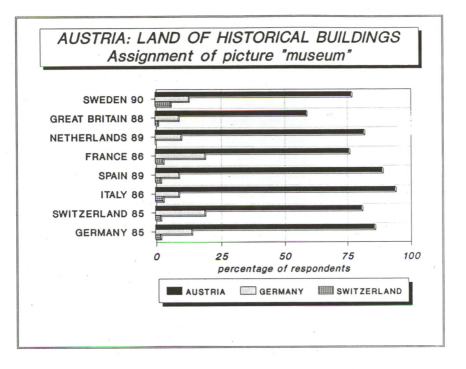

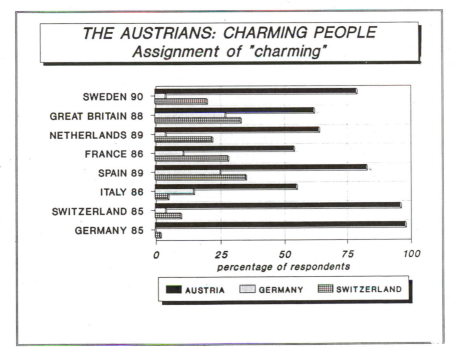

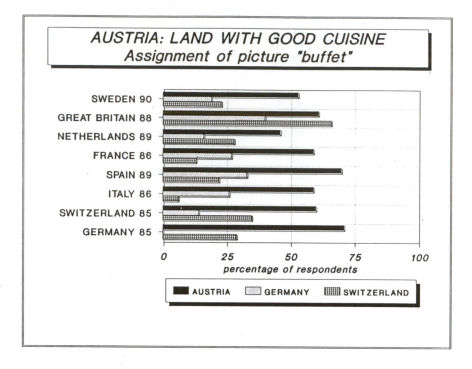

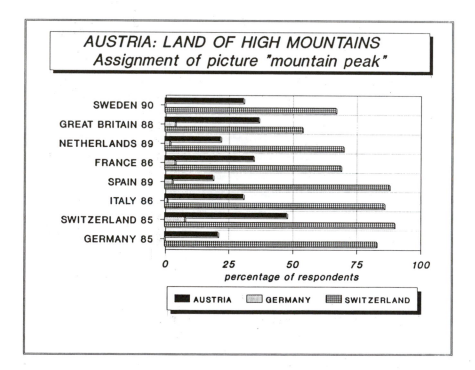

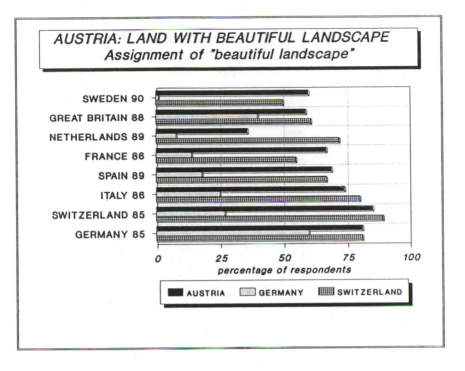

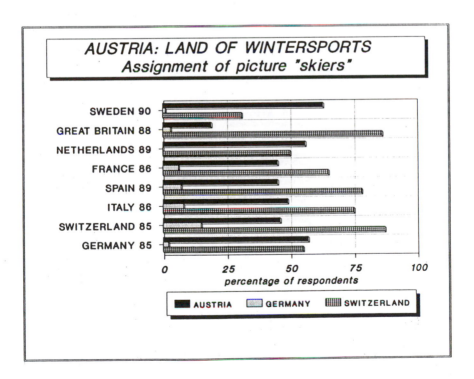

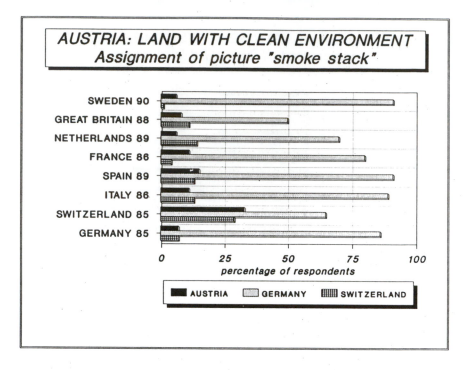

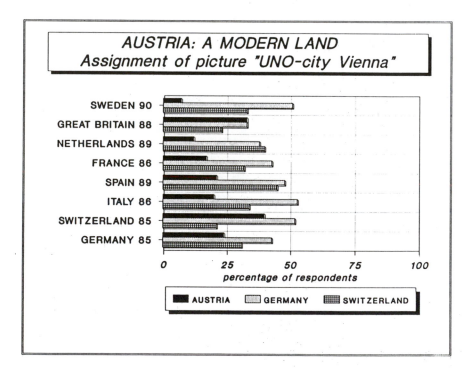

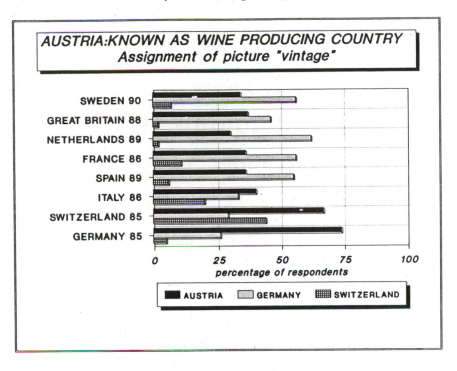

AUSTRIA:KNOWN AS WINE PRODUCING COUNTRY
Assignment of picture "vintage"

percentage of respondents

■ AUSTRIA ▨ GERMANY ▦ SWITZERLAND

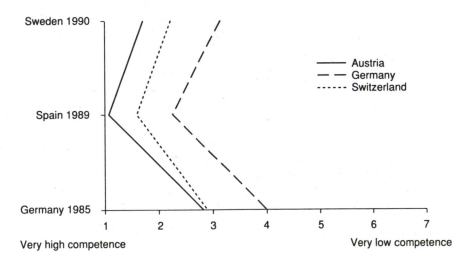

THE COMPETENCE OF SELECTED COUNTRIES:
PRODUCTION OF SKIS

—— Austria
— — Germany
------ Switzerland

Very high competence   Very low competence

Netherlands, Great Britain, France, Italy, Spain and Switzerland: not investigated

10

Copenhagen – City of Culture 1996
Stakeholder analysis

Jesper Christiansen and Kenneth Nielsen

This case illustrates the organizational aspects of marketing in terms of the ways in which different 'stakeholders' or interested parties may bring very different concerns, perspectives and interests to defining and addressing a particular situation.

Copenhagen is to be the European City of Culture in 1996. Many people are interested in this event – the Danish State, the Danish business world, Copenhagen Council and the media, just to mention a few.

Various parties are already involved in the planning of this event and even more will become active participants in the period up to 1996. Depending on which interested party's viewpoint is taken, the issues raised by the event are quite diverse.

This case study offers a glimpse into the background and the aim of the EC's City of Culture project and Copenhagen as the chosen city. Starting with one of the many parties interested in this arrangement, solve the problem. Students are asked to take account of the various perspectives involved in considering the planning and implementation of the event.

Europe's City of Culture: background and aims

The originator of the annual arrangement 'Europe's City of Culture' was the former Minister of Culture for Greece, Melina Mercouri. The idea was launched in 1984, and in 1985 the Ministers of Culture of the EC countries approved Mercouri's proposal for a City of Culture arrangement. Athens was a natural choice as the first City of Culture in 1985, and since then the various member countries have taken turns in hosting 'Europe's City of

Culture'. The City of Culture is chosen by the individual member countries themselves, and the EC Commission contributes an annual symbolic economic contribution of 120,000 ECU to the event. Copenhagen as City of Culture in 1996 ends the first round of the arrangement, which runs from 1985 to 1996. By that time all EC members will have taken turns acting as host. After this it is the intention that other European countries outside the EC will also be chosen to host the City of Culture.

The purpose of this annual event is to demonstrate the chosen cities' cultural characteristics and their relationship to Europe, thereby showing the rest of the world Europe's cultural variety. Furthermore, it is the intention that special aspects of the chosen city's culture are made available for Europeans, especially the population of the city in question.

Experience from former City of Culture arrangements

In spite of the relatively modest economic contribution by the EC Commission to the project, it has become the most important and successful cultural initiative yet taken in connection with the EC. Each year the attention of the world's press is focused on the chosen City of Culture, and this presents a unique opportunity for the city concerned to market itself both nationally, under EC auspices, and globally.

The EC's resolution on the European City of Culture (see Appendix 1) gives the individual organizer very broad scope, which without doubt contributes to the great differences in the many cultural arrangements. The host cities themselves define the concept of culture and decide for themselves how much they shall put into it and in what way. From Exhibit 1 one can clearly see the heterogeneity which characterizes the individual country's choice of themes and targets in connection with hosting the event.

One City of Culture deserves special mention. Glasgow was the city which has had without doubt the greatest success yet. Glasgow, the chosen city in 1990, had a budget of 1.2 billion DDK (Danish kroner): 670 million DDK was connected to the programme and administration, 476 million DDK for investment in construction and 55 million DDK for marketing.[1] This is to date the greatest economic investment, but at the same time it had the effect that Glasgow stands out today as the City of Culture with the greatest success.

Glasgow's target for the year comprised:

- culture aims;
- economic aims;
- social aims.

Because of the very broad formulation of aims, the organizers succeeded in assembling many interested parties in the project. The City of Culture

Exhibit 1   *European Cities of Culture, 1985–92*

Year	City	Target/themes
1985	Athens	**Targets:**

- to relate the culture city to the community
- to involve as many Greek artists as possible
- to bring these artists together with other European artists

(budget: 63 million DDK)

| 1986 | Florence | **Programme:** |

- 'Florence for Europe' had special arrangements in connection with the culture city year
- 'Europe for Florence' was about what Europe could offer the city
- initiatives taken by cultural institutions of Florence with special relevance for Europe

(budget: 174 million DDK)

| 1987 | Amsterdam | **Purpose:** |

- to inform about culture
- to provoke discussion of the importance of culture
- to try to attract more support for export of Dutch culture

(budget: 70 million DDK)

| 1988 | Berlin | **Main themes:** |

- Berlin – the place for innovation
- workshop Berlin
- Berlin in Central Europe

(budget: 250 million DDK)

| 1989 | Paris[1] | (no information available) |

| 1990 | Glasgow | **Targets:** |

- cultural
- economic
- social

(budget: 1.2 billion DDK)

| 1991 | Dublin[2] | **Main themes:** |

- a series of festivals
- exhibitions with separate 'highlights'
- a 'cultural city renewal project' with EC support
- several new cultural institutions, e.g. Irish Museum of Modern Art and Dublin Writers' Museum

(budget: 50 million DDK)

| 1992 | Madrid[3] | **Main themes:** |

- 're-entry' of Spain into Europe; Madrid once again an international city
- 'rediscovery' of the city of Madrid by the people

(budget: 400 million DDK)

Exhibit 1 *continued*

Future culture cities: 1993   Antwerp
1994   Lisbon
1995   Luxembourg
1996   Copenhagen

[1] The 200th anniversary of the French Revolution was celebrated at the same time as the culture city project, and the latter was completely absorbed into the total arrangement.

[2] The expected attention was not attained, presumably owing to the fact that the city celebrated its 1,000th anniversary in 1989.

[3] Despite the ambitious programme, Madrid had difficulty in attracting attention in comparison with other big events, such as Expo '92 and the Olympic Games in Barcelona.

arrangements before Glasgow had all focused on narrow cultural activities for a limited part of the year. In contrast, the activities linked to Glasgow were broadly formulated and spread out over the whole year.

Glasgow's City of Culture project comprised no less than 10,000 events, among them:

1,091   exhibitions
656   theatre performances
3,122   concerts
156   national and international conferences
765   workshops
355   lectures
387   sports arrangements
453   film shows
1,000   organizations, tenant organizations, schools, clubs and local cultural institutions all were involved in a comprehensive programme of local activities with the goal of involving the weaker groups in the community.

Furthermore, large investments were made in building, e.g. rebuilding Glasgow's Royal Concert Hall, restoration of the McLellan Galleries and the opening of a new multimedia centre, The Tramway.

The outcome of the event was a strong growth in the cultural sector and an increase in the flow of tourists; this resulted in the creation of 5,500 new jobs.

As can be seen from the above, Glasgow is clear proof of the great opportunities connected to hosting the City of Culture. In Denmark, Glasgow is repeatedly held up as the perfect example of success and an ideal model to follow in 1996.

Copenhagen as City of Culture

In Denmark today, there is an increasing awareness from a political point of view of the importance of tourism. In recent years especially, the focus has been on improving and developing Denmark's capital with the aim of making Copenhagen a cultural tourist attraction.

For this reason, it is an obvious opportunity for Copenhagen, as the City of Culture in 1996, to give it the cultural 'lift' needed, so as to realize some of the many plans and ideas for the city that the politicians have had in the past. More and more people are becoming aware of the unique possibilities which the cultural year could offer in this respect.

Initiatives have already been taken. At the moment 383 million DDK has been set aside in the budget for Copenhagen for 1996; this money is thus assured for the cultural project. A similar sum of nearly 400 million DDK is expected to be approved during the present year. Sources point out that approval is only a matter of form, as all the economic and cultural representatives of the political parties have reached an agreement to grant this money. Thus, there is now almost 800 million DDK set aside for the project.

Apart from this, there is an estimated surplus of 750 million DDK derived from the sale of the new 'Tøjhus' site. This money can perhaps be included as capital for the project, according to Henning Dyremose, former Minister of Finance.

For a further supply of capital, there is the intention to involve large parts of the private sector, in the hope that the business world may wish to sponsor the project. Negotiations are under way at the moment with the ATP fund (Supplementary Labour Market Pension Fund) and the Employees Cost of Living Fund about their potential participation in or contribution to the 'City of Culture '96'.

How should the money be used? The following initiatives have been suggested:

- building an opera house or theatre;
- extending the Royal Theatre;
- a multi-centre with trade as the primary interest;
- a multi-house – an Eldorado for the arts à la Pompidou in Paris;
- a new art museum (160 million DDK);
- enlarging the Tøjhus museum (160 million DDK);
- extending the Royal Library (340 million DDK);
- a new centre in Copenhagen for education in the arts;
- building attractive housing (200 million DDK);
- assembling the buildings of Copenhagen Business School into one building.

There is no absolute agreement on what is to be built and where. The answer depends on who is asked. In other words, there is a high level of diversity in the aims and interests of those concerned in the project.

The following districts and boroughs have taken on some of the responsibilities of the cultural project: Copenhagen Council, Frederiksberg Council, the County of Frederiksborg and the County of Roskilde.

For this purpose, the Copenhagen City of Culture Fund '96 has been set up. It consists of:

- the management;
- the committee;
- the ideas board;
- the secretariat.

The secretariat was established in the autumn of 1991, and its activities are, like those of the other parties in the fund, exclusively connected to the cultural event in 1996. The secretariat has the main responsibility for co-ordinating and completing the final programme for 1996. In addition to being responsible for working out the framework of the project, the secretariat will also be responsible for information on and marketing of the event.

The ideas board, which has an advisory function to the secretariat, must cross the traditional professional boundaries and methods of work and explore the new and unexpected. In other words, the ideas board will function as a kind of 'think tank' and forum for ideas. The ideas board consists of representatives from the authorities and from the cultural and social life in the Copenhagen district.

The regulations of the Copenhagen City of Culture Fund '96 include the following:

> The purpose of the Fund is to plan and give support to the accomplishment of arrangements and projects in connection with Copenhagen as the City of Culture 1996.

> The arrangements and projects shall contribute to enhancing the cultural identity and status of Copenhagen and present Copenhagen as a city with human dimensions where culture is an integrated part of daily life.

> The arrangements and projects can in part be specific and temporary, and in part establish permanent cultural activities, so that the cultural milieu of Copenhagen will be enhanced, not only in 1996, but also in the future.

> To the extent possible, it is presupposed that the arrangements and projects are established through broad collaboration with, among others, public institutions, trade, and the people living in and/or frequenting the city.

Diverse 'problem definitions': an interest-party model

In this context of so many different interested parties, or stakeholders, the question of what should be the specific aims and objectives of the Copenhagen City of Culture event, and how these should be addressed, is not a straightforward matter. Exhibit 2 shows an interest-party model of the potential stakeholders involved.

Each of these parties may define the situation in different ways.

Exhibit 2   *Copenhagen 1996: interest-party model of potential stakeholders*

Furthermore, each could in turn comprise a number of sub-interest groups. For example, taking the state as one interest party, this could be subdivided into a large number of sub-groups, such as the various political parties, the Ministry of Culture and the Ministry of Finance. Each of these sub-parties could again have more or less different concerns and perspectives from the others, and thus more or less different 'problem definitions'.

Thus unemployment is currently a major macro-economic problem for Denmark. For the Ministry of Finance the City of Culture event could represent a means of attracting investment and creating new jobs both within the cultural and other business sectors.

Any analyst working with such a situation would need to understand the different situational and problem definitions of the parties concerned, as the basis for identifying key points of diversity and commonality and in order to develop appropriate plans for the implementation of the City of Culture event reflecting these.

Questions for discussion/suggested tasks

1   Are there any alternative/complementary ways of completing and/or representing the interest-party model shown in Exhibit 2?
2   Identify the potential aims and interests of the various interest parties with respect to the Copenhagen City of Culture event, including the issues likely to be perceived as significant by the secretariat of the City of Culture Fund.
3   Assume that one of the aims and concerns of the City of Culture Fund is to use the event as a means of increasing domestic tourism to Copenhagen. Using the information provided in Appendix 2:

   (a) Identify target segments within the Danish population for the design and marketing of the City of Culture event as one way of attracting increased domestic tourism to Copenhagen, during the City of Culture year and thereafter.
   (b) Consider how you would design and market the event to attract these target segments.

4   Take another EC country with which you are familiar and also (a) identify appropriate target groups for increased tourism to Copenhagen, and (b) plan a marketing campaign designed to attract these groups to visit Copenhagen during the City of Culture year and thereafter.

Note

1. 1 DDK is approximately 0.17 US dollars.

Appendix 1: Text of the EC City of Culture resolution

RESOLUTION

of the Ministers responsible for Cultural Affairs, meeting within

the Council, of 13 June 1985

concerning the annual event 'European City of Culture'

(85/C 153/02)

I   Aim and content

The Ministers responsible for Cultural Affairs consider that the 'European City of Culture' event should be the expression of a culture which, in its historical emergence and contemporary development, is characterized by having both common elements and a richness born of diversity. The event has been established to help bring the peoples of the Member States closer together, but account should be taken of wider European cultural affinities.

The event should open up to the European public particular aspects of the culture of the city, region or country concerned. It may also concentrate on the city concerned a number of cultural contributions from other Member States, primarily for the benefit of the inhabitants of the particular region. Between these two poles, a wide variety of emphases can be placed and interrelated themes chosen so as to enhance the city concerned and mark the particular occasion, if any, which has provided a reason for choosing it.

II Selection criteria

As a general rule, only one 'European City of Culture' should be chosen each calendar year. Each year one Member State should hold the event. The decision on the choice of city must be taken at least two years in advance, so as to allow proper arrangements to be made. The Member States should in principle follow each other in alphabetical order. They may, however, alter the chronological order of events by agreement.

In principle, one round of the Member States should be completed before another one is begun.

III Organization and finance

The Member State in which the designated 'European City of Culture' lies decides which authority inside the Member State will take responsibility for organizing and financing the event.

Given that the event forms part of cultural cooperation among the Member States, these should be associated with its preparation and kept regularly informed of progress. Other European and, where appropriate, non-European countries may also be associated with the preparation of the event. Ministers responsible for Cultural Affairs in the Member States should if possible attend the opening ceremony.

Member States should take all possible steps to publicize the event widely.

Appendix 2: Data on Denmark

Table 1 Attendance at cultural and sporting activities, 1981–91

Museums (visitors, thousand)	1981	1982	1983	1984	1985	1986	1987	1988	1989	1990	1991
National museum with affiliated museum	1,110	1,016	1,045	1,015	951	782	451[1]	807	637	511	418
Historical local museums	1,756	1,670	1,646	1,738	1,854	1,787	1,732	1,732	1,859	2,017	2,289
Historical specialized museums	3,366	3,146	3,071	3,129	3,361	3,371	3,042	3,730	3,561	4,077	3,808
Art museums	1,922	1,778	2,054	1,777	2,005	1,892	1,978	2,102	2,305	2,524	2,313
Natural science museums	386	449	415	398	367	377	367	422	408	361	352
Zoological gardens, etc.	1,850	1,596	1,804	1,899	1,833	1,795	1,871	1,800	1,800	1,762	1,641

Sport and outdoor life (active members, thousand)	1980	1981	1982	1983	1984	1985	1986	1987	1988	1989	1990
Danish Athletics League	1,310	1,339	1,387	1,408	1,428	1,468	1,473	1,509	1,542	1,542	1,528
Danish Gymnastics and Youth Leagues	854	869	870	851	888	895	877	854	877	897	896
Danish Sharpshooting, Gymnastics and Athletics Leagues	763	758	773	788	783	796	807	827	825	846	868
Danish Company Sports Leagues	159	160	163	169	167	171	182	185	195	204	208
Children and Youth Organization Confederations (scouts corps, etc.)	138	136	136	144	146	143	134	130	131	133	134

Films	1981	1982	1983	1984	1985	1986	1987	1988	1989	1990	1991
Films shown in a cinema (total)	2,174	2,125	2,009	1,625	1,566	1,377	1,182	1,216	1,027	841	771
Danish films	326	300	269	242	233	216	214	215	211	186	172
Foreign films	1,848	1,825	1,740	1,383	1,333	1,161	968	1,001	816	655	599
Of these, total premiered this year	263	267	244	209	227	220	219	241	201	172	147
Danish films	17	8	11	11	10	10	12	16	16	13	11
Foreign films	246	259	233	198	217	210	207	225	185	159	136

Continued

Table 1   *continued*

Cinemas	*1981*	*1982*	*1983*	*1984*	*1985*	*1986*	*1987*	*1988*	*1989*	*1990*	*1991*
No. of cinemas in 4th quarter	310	295	276	265	241	221	207	195	187	180	176
Of these, multi-house cinemas	85	88	93	92	94	89	89	86	77	73	69
No. of permanent cinemas in 4th quarter	471	463	453	449	429	406	397	381	358	347	334
Of these, multi-house cinemas	246	256	270	276	282	275	280	272	248	240	228
Permanent seats (thousand)	103	98	92	86	76	70	67	63	59	57	58
No. of sold tickets (thousand)	16,208	14,272	13,825	11,787	11,278	11,355	11,448	9,962	10,255	9,624	9,218
Of these, for Danish films	4,101	2,995	2,830	2,754	2,193	2,841	2,435	1,906	1,705	1,640	1,204

Theatres (season 1 July–30 June)	*1980–1*	*1981–2*	*1982–3*	*1983–4*	*1984–5*	*1985–6*	*1986–7*	*1987–8*	*1988–9*	*1989–90*	*1990–1*
Royal Theatre											
No. of performances	786	805	611	610	697	621	600	746	652	562	690
Audience (thousand)	521	494	421	351	395	379	393	391	384	374	379
Greater Copenhagen Touring Company											
No. of performances	2,258	2,261	1,906	1,778	1,840	1,699	1,728	1,724	1,264	1,300	1,178
Audience (thousand)	801	914	801	756	727	676	674	642	484	536	518
Touring companies in the provinces											
No. of performances	1,222	1,130	1,243	1,125	1,116	1,085	1,025	962	967	1,073	940
Audience (thousand)	402	360	351	371	370	319	282	273	245	279	271
Other state-subsidized theatres[2]											
No. of performances	6,973	7,798	7,136	6,214	7,106	6,912	6,786	6,838	7,303	7,114	7,409
Audience (thousand)	982	1,179	1,151	1,044	1,278	1,209	1,106	1,097	1,113	1,112	1,081
State-subsidized theatres in all											
Audience (thousand)	2,706	2,947	2,724	2,522	2,770	2,583	2,455	2,403	2,226	2,301	2,249

[1] Closed because of strike 1 April 88–17 August 88.
[2] The touring Landsteater, the touring children's theatre, regional theatres and theatres receiving subsidies according to para. 15, 16c, 17 and 18 in the theatre law.

Source: Danmarks Statistik

Table 2   Participation in cultural and outdoor activities during the year to March 1991 (%)

		Have participated in the past year			Have not participated in the past year
	Total	1–2 times	3–5 times	6 or more times	
Library attendance	55	7	10	38	45
Books read[1]	71	10	17	44	29
Cinema attendance	45	17	14	14	55
Art museum attendance	37	19	12	6	63
Other museum attendance	38	23	10	5	62
Classical concert attendance	15	8	4	3	85
Rock concert attendance	19	10	6	3	81
Jazz/folksong concert attendance	18	12	3	3	82
Theatre attendance	31	19	8	4	69

	Total	Once a month	2–3 times a month	Once a week	Have not participated
Spectator at sports contests, and similar	28	19	6	3	72
Participant in sports contests, and similar	16	7	2	7	84
Take active part in sports or exercise[2]	43	2	3	38	57
Take long walks or cycle long distances	67	5	5	57	33

Sample: $n = 1,106$ (interviews)

[1] 'Easy-reader' books.

[2] The question was: 'Do you usually take exercise or train in any way other than walking or cycling for long distances?'

Source: Danmarks Statistik

Table 3   Proportion of the population who go to various cultural events, by age and sex, 1987 (%)

	Cinema[1]	Theatre[2]	Art exhibition/ museum[3]	Other museum[3]	Classical concert[3]	Jazz/ rock concert[3]
16–24 age group	53	36	32	30	9	46
25–34 age group	30	39	34	33	9	30
35–44 age group	21	43	46	42	12	17
45–54 age group	12	41	41	35	18	8
55–64 age group	8	31	34	26	14	3
65–74 age group	7	25	33	26	13	–
Total	24	37	37	33	12	20
Men	25	34	34	33	11	23
Women	23	40	40	35	14	17

[1] Within the past month.

[2] Within the past six months.

[3] Within the past year.

Source: Danmarks Statistik

Table 4 *Proportion of the population who go to various cultural events, by socio-economic group, 1987 (%)*

	Cinema[1]	Theatre[2]	Art exhibition/ museum[3]	Other museum[3]	Classical concert[3]	Jazz/ rock concert[3]
Farmers	4	31	26	23	9	7
Other self-employed	16	36	39	29	17	12
Assisting spouses	4	41	31	38	10	7
Salaried employees, upper level	18	49	60	53	21	19
Salaried employees, intermediate level	27	50	51	46	15	23
Salaried employees, lower level	29	47	43	41	15	27
Skilled manual workers	32	24	20	26	5	25
Unskilled manual workers	17	24	15	18	4	11
Unemployed[4]	28	27	34	31	10	24
Students	60	50	54	45	15	57
Pensioners	7	26	31	25	11	2
Housewives	11	25	34	25	11	3
Total	24	37	37	34	12	20

[1] Within the past month.
[2] Within the past six months.
[3] Within the past year.
[4] People who at the time of interview had been unemployed for more than one month.

Source: Danmarks Statistik

Table 5 *Holidaying in Denmark and abroad, socio-demographic factors, 1990 (%)*

	Total	Holidayed in Denmark	Holidayed abroad	Non-travellers
Sex				
Male	52	52	53	49
Female	48	48	47	51
Age				
16–19 years	7	6	9	5
20–29 years	20	19	20	20
30–39 years	18	24	16	16
40–49 years	18	22	20	14
50–59 years	13	11	14	11
60–69 years	12	9	11	15
70 or more	12	8	10	19
Civilian status				
Unmarried	22	20	24	22
Married/cohabiting	61	66	61	56
Previously married	8	8	6	9
Widow/widower	9	7	8	13
Education				
General education				
without vocational education	24	20	17	35
Upper secondary education	45	48	43	45
Student higher education	14	17	17	10
Higher education	8	8	11	5
Student	9	7	12	5
Social level				
1 (high)	20	24	26	10
2	13	15	14	11
3	20	23	18	19
4	19	16	18	21
5 (low)	13	11	7	21
Don't know/no answer	(15)	(12)	(16)	(17)
Children				
(under 16 years)				
None	69	54	73	74
0–16 years	31	46	27	26
Total number (thousand)	4,183	956	1,803	1,424

Source: Danish Travel Analysis, 1991

Table 6 Main reasons for spending the longest holiday abroad in 1990 (%)

	Total	Age			Social level			Child/children		
		16–29	30–49	50–69	1–2 High	3	4–5 Low	None	0–6	7–15
Climate/weather/sun/heat	27	30	28	24	28	30	23	26	29	28
Beach/water/seaside holiday	4	4	3	3	4	4	3	3	4	4
Low cost in general	11	13	11	9	12	13	12	11	12	12
Low living expenses	1	0	1	1	1	2	1	1	0	1
Like the people/good local population	4	3	3	5	4	5	3	4	1	3
Good atmosphere	2	2	2	2	2	3	2	2	1	2
Went with family/friends/acquaintances	5	6	4	5	4	4	6	5	5	4
See/experience foreign countries/culture/surroundings	32	33	29	33	30	32	31	33	24	29
Visited family/friends/acquaintances at the same time	14	14	14	13	14	13	15	14	19	12
Have summer/holiday home abroad	1	0	1	1	1	0	0	1	0	1
In connection with sports meeting	1	2	1	1	1	3	1	1	2	1
Was invited/was given the trip	3	3	2	2	2	1	4	3	1	2
Study trip/course/seminar/class trip	3	8	1	1	2	5	4	3	2	3
Skiing holiday/snow	5	6	8	1	7	3	4	4	8	8
Beautiful/magnificent scenery/mountains	9	6	11	12	8	10	11	9	10	11
Safari/animals	0	0	0	0	0	0	0	0	0	0
Borrowed summer/holiday home/sailboat	1	1	2	1	2	1	1	1	1	2
Exotic/different food	1	2	1	1	1	1	2	1	1	1
Exotic sights	1	1	1	1	1	1	1	1	0	1
Combined business and holiday	2	2	3	2	3	2	1	2	2	1
Handicap – possibility for trip with lift bus	0	0	0	0	0	0	0	0	0	0
Because of a special event	2	1	2	3	3	1	1	3	1	1

Table 6 *continued*

	Total	Age			Social level			Child/children		
		16–29	30–49	50–69	1–2 High	3	4–5 Low	None	0–6	7–15
Wanted to try travelling abroad	2	2	2	2	2	2	2	2	4	2
Wine tasting holiday/wine interest	1	0	1	0	1	0	0	0	1	1
Inter-rail	0	0	0	0	0	0	0	0	0	0
Long-held desire to go there	0	0	0	1	1	0	0	0	0	0
Shopping trip/to buy certain things	0	0	0	0	0	0	0	0	0	0
Wanted to see/know an Eastern bloc country	1	1	1	1	1	1	1	1	1	2
In Denmark in the summer and abroad when cold here	0	0	0	0	0	0	0	0	0	0
Have always holidayed abroad	1	1	1	1	1	1	1	1	2	1
Not known	1	0	1	0	0	1	1	1	0	1
Number asked	1,755	508	634	443	709	319	449	1,278	214	351
Total number (thousand)	1,803	522	651	455	728	328	461	1,313	220	361

Source: Danish Travel Analysis, 1991

Table 7 *Main reasons for spending the longest holiday in Denmark in 1990 (%)*

	Total	Age			Social level			Child/children		
		16–29	30–49	50–69	1–2 High	3	4–5 Low	None	0–6	7–15
Like DK/prefer holiday in DK	24	18	26	26	24	22	25	25	19	25
Should see own country/children should see DK first	9	8	12	9	9	11	9	7	11	13
Danish climate/weather	5	6	6	3	6	6	4	6	3	5
Close to home/short journey	3	1	2	4	2	2	4	4	1	2
Family reasons	5	3	5	4	4	5	5	4	4	5
Economy/cheap holiday	30	44	30	17	31	34	27	27	35	30
Have summer/holiday home in DK	7	3	7	14	7	8	5	9	4	5
Beautiful scenery	7	4	10	6	9	7	6	7	6	10
Visited family/friends/acquaintances at same time	15	20	11	18	12	15	20	18	13	12
Wanted to see all the Scandinavian countries incl. DK	—	—	—	1	—	—	—	1	—	1
Could bring domestic animals (dog/cat)	1	1	1	1	1	1	2	1	—	1
Stayed in DK because of illness	2	1	1	6	1	2	5	1	1	1
Went to summer school/course/scouts	2	2	1	2	1	5	3	4	1	1
Canoeing/bathing holiday	1	1	2	1	2	1	—	1	—	1
Could borrow a summer home/caravan	5	7	4	4	5	4	4	4	1	2
Abroad strenuous with small children	7	5	11	1	11	5	3	4	23	9
Get to know Danish culture/history	1	1	—	1	1	—	1	—	—	—
Wanted to try a holiday in DK	1	—	1	1	1	1	1	1	1	2
Holiday in connection with sports meeting	1	1	1	2	1	1	1	1	—	1
Place recommended/popular place	1	1	—	1	—	1	—	1	—	—
Because of special event	1	2	1	2	2	—	2	2	1	—
Not known	1	1	—	—	1	—	—	1	1	1
Number asked	931	241	424	191	361	213	247	507	226	293
Total number (thousand)	956	248	436	196	371	219	254	521	232	301

Source: Danish Travel Analysis, 1991

Table 8 *Domestic holiday destination, by countries, 1987 and 1990 (%)*

	1987	1990
Bornholm County	8	7
North Zealand County	7	7
Borough and County Copenhagen	4	4
Central Zealand County	7	9
South Zealand County (Lolland/Falster/Møn)	7	6
Funen County (Langeland/Tåsinge/Aerø)	9	9
South Jutland County	6	6
East Jutland County	16	16
Central Jutland County	4	2
West Coast (Rømø to Limfjorden)	7	11
Region around Limfjorden	5	4
North Jutland County	19	21
Total holidays (thousand)	1,302	1,515

The questions were: 'Here is a list with a number of Danish counties. Which of these counties did you visit for the longest period during your longest holiday in 1987?' and 'Do you remember the destination of your second and eventually third holiday in 1990 (duration of at least 5 days/bed-nights)?'

Sources: Danish Travel Analysis, 1988 and 1991

Table 9 *Travel motives for most important holiday in 1987 and 1990 (%)*

	Total		Denmark		Abroad	
	1987	1990	1987	1990	1987	1990
Clean air and water/away from pollution	46	46	52	56	43	40
Eat well	43	42	38	38	46	44
Spoil oneself/enjoy life/be waited upon	45	43	39	40	48	44
Be with other people/social life	38	35	35	34	39	36
Travel around a lot/be on the move	25	25	14	14	30	32
Get out of the shell and take a chance/try something new	22	22	15	15	26	25
Get away from the daily round	70	63	72	67	68	61
See other countries/the world outside	49	50	11	12	68	70
Get to know the local population	31	30	20	18	37	38
See family, friends and acquaintances	37	33	53	43	29	27
Fun and entertainment/amusement	33	29	31	30	33	29
Many experiences/variety	59	58	43	42	67	68
Get away/relax	66	58	70	68	64	53
Peace and quiet/not do anything	33	28	39	35	30	24
Do something for one's appearance/get sun tan	27	18	25	17	28	19
Take active part in sports	10	10	8	9	11	11
Experience something cultural	26	28	18	20	30	33
Enjoy nature	67	67	72	71	65	64
Enjoy the sun/escape from bad weather	48	37	29	27	58	42
Do what one likes/to be free	75	75	73	80	76	73
Cultivate my hobby/favourite occupation	17	18	21	21	15	16
Have time for each other	72	71	80	80	68	68
Do something for one's health/prevent illnesses	21	18	22	21	20	16
Refresh memories of place/area/region	26	24	33	27	22	23

Number asked: 2,782 in 1987; 2,759 in 1990

Source: Danish Travel Analysis, 1991

Table 10 *Travel motives for most important holiday in 1987 and 1990, by sex, age, status and region of Denmark (%)*

	Total	Sex		Age							Status				Danish region		
		Male	Female	16–19	20–9	30–9	40–9	50–9	60–9	70–9	Un-married	Married	Previously married	Widowed	West	Middle	East
Clean air and water/away from pollution	46	44	47	39	44	51	45	46	47	44	40	48	47	40	43	48	47
Eat well	42	43	41	33	43	42	39	48	45	44	39	42	44	49	41	43	43
Spoil oneself/enjoy life/be waited upon	43	38	47	34	45	41	43	43	45	45	40	44	43	45	41	51	43
Be with other people/social life	35	34	37	59	45	23	26	28	38	49	54	26	46	50	35	43	35
Travel around a lot/be on the move	25	25	26	35	28	18	21	27	29	29	32	23	26	29	24	32	25
Get out of the shell and take a chance/try something new	22	19	24	42	28	16	17	19	18	19	34	17	31	19	21	27	21
Get away from the daily round	63	60	65	54	66	65	65	62	54	65	59	63	67	65	61	72	62
See other countries/the world outside	50	47	54	59	51	36	50	57	59	50	55	48	52	51	50	54	50

Continued

Table 10 *continued*

	Total	Sex		Age							Status				Danish region		
		Male	Female	16–19	20–9	30–9	40–9	50–9	60–9	70–9	Un-married	Married	Previously married	Wid-owed	West	Middle	East
Get to know the local population	30	26	34	29	26	20	33	38	36	34	30	28	42	34	29	31	30
See family, friends and acquaintances	33	28	37	29	38	29	28	33	38	35	35	31	34	38	31	30	34
Fun and entertainment/ amusement	29	30	29	72	50	24	18	15	19	18	57	21	28	20	29	39	28
Many experiences/ variety	58	55	60	67	60	50	56	58	61	62	63	55	59	63	59	64	56
Get away/relax	58	59	58	37	55	69	68	59	49	48	46	64	55	47	56	60	59
Peace and quiet/not do anything	28	28	28	21	20	28	31	34	33	30	20	31	27	29	29	27	27
Do something for one's appearance/ get sun tan	18	15	21	21	18	14	19	19	23	19	20	17	25	21	19	20	17
Take active part in sports	10	12	9	17	11	13	11	7	5	5	14	9	10	5	9	10	11
Experience something cultural	28	24	33	29	22	16	29	37	37	45	27	26	39	43	26	28	31
Enjoy nature	67	62	70	40	54	70	69	75	81	75	49	72	70	73	66	77	65

Enjoy the sun/escape from bad weather	37	35	39	35	39	33	37	37	34	41	37	37	38	37	35	36	38
Do what one likes/to be free	75	74	76	67	82	80	78	74	61	69	75	77	75	62	75	77	75
Cultivate my hobby/favourite occupation	18	20	16	25	18	18	18	19	14	15	22	16	21	16	17	17	19
Have time for each other	71	69	72	58	69	83	80	70	51	62	53	80	66	48	73	76	68
Do something for one's health/prevent illnesses	18	16	19	8	10	15	21	21	26	29	10	19	25	22	17	22	18
Refresh memories of place/area/region	24	21	27	20	17	18	23	30	39	34	19	25	32	33	22	26	26
Not known	1	1	0	1	1	0	1	–	1	–	1	0	–	1	1	–	0
Number asked	2,686	1,268	1,418	224	525	509	549	355	245	279	610	1,691	183	202	1,176	218	1,292
Total number (thousand)	2,759	1,303	1,457	230	539	532	564	365	252	287	627	1,737	188	208	1,208	224	1,327

Source: Danish Travel Analysis, 1991

Table 11 Travel motives for most important holiday in 1987 and 1990, by education and occupation (%)

	Total	Own education					Occupation									Car	
		Primary school 9 years upper secondary	Primary school 10+ years higher secondary	Upper secondary	Higher	Student	Farmer	Other self-employed	Wife working in husband's enterprise	Office worker, civil servant	Manual worker	House-wife	Student/school pupil	Pen-sioner	Un-employed	Yes	No
Clean air and water/away from pollution	46	47	50	45	29	41	31	46	64	44	53	47	38	48	49	46	45
Eat well	42	50	47	31	34	33	40	44	50	40	48	35	33	46	48	41	45
Spoil oneself/enjoy life/be waited upon	43	47	49	34	33	33	40	42	41	43	49	47	32	46	40	42	45
Be with other people/social life	35	43	35	25	22	53	29	24	36	26	39	35	54	44	37	31	46
Travel around a lot/be on the move	25	26	23	26	22	37	24	25	27	23	20	16	37	30	24	24	28
Get out of the shell and take a chance/try something new	22	23	22	16	14	35	21	22	18	18	24	23	34	20	24	19	27
Get away from the daily round	63	69	67	56	49	56	69	60	59	62	69	63	56	63	68	62	64
See other countries/the world outside	50	50	47	53	51	59	50	50	59	50	42	49	60	53	45	49	54

	1	2	3	4	5	6	7	8	9	10	11	12	13	14	15	16	17
Get to know the local population	30	34	29	29	30	30	24	28	41	29	25	37	30	37	24	29	33
See family, friends and acquaintances	33	36	33	28	30	34	17	32	55	29	33	42	31	38	38	30	38
Fun and entertainment/amusement	29	28	31	15	16	59	21	19	32	21	38	19	60	19	41	26	38
Many experiences/variety	58	62	56	56	56	65	50	49	55	54	58	67	66	61	60	57	60
Get away/relax	58	55	62	62	56	42	62	62	55	66	62	70	40	50	52	61	52
Peace and quiet/not do anything	28	33	31	25	21	17	36	27	50	28	31	30	15	34	25	29	26
Do something for one's appearance/get sun tan	18	25	21	12	7	17	14	10	27	16	23	23	16	23	14	18	19
Take active part in sports	10	7	10	10	11	19	2	13	9	11	9	12	18	5	9	10	10
Experience something cultural	28	26	25	36	34	30	17	30	50	25	22	35	32	41	22	26	33
Enjoy nature	67	75	69	67	61	47	64	67	68	66	69	74	47	78	70	68	63
Enjoy the sun/escape from bad weather	37	37	41	33	26	37	26	33	64	36	41	40	35	37	34	37	37
Do what one likes/to be free	75	72	81	76	60	69	62	70	77	79	82	77	69	66	80	76	73

Continued

Table 11 *continued*

	Own education						Occupation									Car	
	Total	Primary school 9 years upper secondary	Primary school 10+ years higher	Upper secondary	Higher	Student	Farmer	Other self-employed	Wife working in husband's enterprise	Office worker, civil servant	Manual worker	House-wife	Student/school pupil	Pen-sioner	Un-employed	Yes	No
Cultivate my hobby/favourite occupation	18	14	17	19	21	26	14	18	18	16	18	23	26	16	18	18	17
Have time for each other	71	66	76	72	66	58	62	74	86	77	76	79	57	58	74	74	63
Do something for one's health/prevent illnesses	18	23	19	16	12	12	5	21	50	15	18	26	9	28	20	19	15
Refresh memories of place/area/region	24	32	25	21	20	16	17	18	23	21	26	30	17	38	26	24	25
Not known	1	1	0	0	1	2	–	–	–	1	0	–	2	0	–	1	0
Number asked	2,686	493	1,201	452	257	279	42	103	22	1,085	416	43	334	476	164	1,853	833
Total number (thousand)	2,759	506	1,234	464	264	287	43	106	23	1,115	427	44	343	489	168	1,904	856

Source: Danish Travel Analysis 1991

Table 12 Reasons given for not travelling, by age and social group (%)

	Not travelled 1988–90	Not travelled in 1990	Not travelled in 1990 Age 16–29	Age 30–40	Age 50–60	Social level 1–2	Social level 3	Social level 4–5
Usually stay at home	27	17	11	16	24	11	16	21
For health reasons	24	19	2	9	23	6	9	29
Low finances	23	24	36	31	17	22	30	24
Home is best	21	14	5	11	23	7	13	18
Not very interested in travel	20	13	7	10	18	7	14	15
Limited time because of work	14	13	22	17	8	21	20	6
Because of general uncertainty	14	13	20	12	14	9	14	14
Because of small children	10	10	16	16	3	18	10	5
Because of old age	10	7	1	0	5	0	4	11
Not had holiday of more than 5 days in 1990	10	10	10	9	11	9	9	10
Spend money on other things for once	8	9	12	10	10	6	13	9
Expensive holiday last year/ planned holiday next year	1	2	4	2	2	3	1	2
Made large economic purchases (house, car etc.) instead	8	10	18	14	4	19	12	6
Consideration for the family	6	7	7	7	8	7	7	7
Because of unemployment	3	3	4	4	2	2	3	3
Because of uncertain employment/ part-time work	2	2	3	3	1	3	2	2

Source: Danish Travel Analysis, 1991

Table 13　Attitudes on holidays generally (%)

	Agree				Disagree			
	Total	Holidayed in Denmark in 1990	Holidayed abroad in 1990	Non-travelling	Total	Holidayed in Denmark in 1990	Holidayed abroad in 1990	Non-travelling
I wish first and foremost to be with my family/children when on holiday	65	76	58	68	19	15	24	17
I prefer that my holiday is completely organized (package deal) or partly organized by a travel bureau rather than arranging it myself	34	26	34	41	47	58	49	38
I am can make do with less comfort during my holiday than at home	67	73	65	60	18	15	18	21
One of my greatest dreams is to travel around for a year	35	31	41	29	50	54	44	56
I want to relax and not do anything during my holiday	40	44	33	44	43	38	50	37
On my holiday I want to experience as much as possible	75	70	78	75	9	12	7	10
Total number (thousand)	4,183	956	1,803	1,424	4,183	956	1,803	1,424

The question was: 'On the list there are a number of everyday opinions on holidays. How far do you agree with the opinions in question?' 'Agree' = 'completely agree' and 'agree on the whole'. 'Disagree' = 'completely disagree' and 'disagree on the whole'. Respondents could also answer 'neither/nor', which corresponds to a 'don't know' and is not included in the table.
Number asked: 4,072

Source: Danish Travel Analysis, 1991

Table 14 Attitudes on holidays in Denmark (%)

	Agree						Disagree					
	Total		Holidayed in Denmark		Holidayed abroad		Total		Holidayed in Denmark		Holidayed abroad	
	1987	1990	1987	1990	1987	1990	1987	1990	1987	1990	1987	1990
Opinions on price												
For the cost of a holiday in Denmark I can get far more value for money abroad	39	34	27	21	49	43	26	35	39	48	22	31
It is possible to have a good and cheap holiday in Denmark	80	80	91	90	74	75	8	8	4	5	11	11
Opinions on weather												
The weather is too unstable to spend holidays in Denmark	31	24	19	15	41	29	48	48	64	72	38	56
One can have a holiday in Denmark and do many exciting things even if the sun isn't shining	90	91	97	95	87	87	4	4	2	1	7	5
The Danish climate is not so bad, but quite pleasant and varied	63	73	73	81	52	66	17	10	9	7	24	15
Opinions on experiences												
There are in fact many sights/ holiday attractions in Denmark	91	90	95	93	89	89	3	3	1	1	3	4

Continued

Table 14 *continued*

	Agree						Disagree					
	Total		Holidayed in Denmark		Holidayed abroad		Total		Holidayed in Denmark		Holidayed abroad	
	1987	1990	1987	1990	1987	1990	1987	1990	1987	1990	1987	1990
Denmark is not different enough for me to stay at home	11	13	6	6	15	17	75	75	87	88	68	67
The scenery in this country is not very exciting	12	11	7	8	14	14	80	80	87	86	77	78
The aqualands are one of the new offers which make a holiday in Denmark attractive		29		32		24		37		32		45
I prefer holiday in Denmark because of the clean environment		29		35		20		28		20		46

The question was: 'One can have different opinions on spending a holiday in Denmark. Some of these questions are on the list. How far do you agree with the opinions in question?'

'Agree' = 'completely agree' or 'agree on the whole'. 'Disagree' = 'completely disagree' or 'disagree on the whole'.
Total number asked: 4,077

Source: Danish Travel Analysis, 1991

Table 15 Sources of holiday information, 1990 (%)

	Total	Hol. in Denmark	Hol. abroad	Age			Social level			Child/children		
				16–29	30–49	50–69	1–2 High	3	4–5 Low	None	0–6	7–15
Recommended by family/friends/ acquaintances	32	28	35	43	28	29	29	35	36	34	30	29
A travel bureau	9	3	13	10	8	10	8	8	11	10	6	9
Brochure from countries/destination	9	4	12	9	10	9	11	8	6	8	9	12
Danish tourist office of destination	3	2	3	3	3	3	3	3	2	2	4	3
Local tourist office in DK/abroad	5	7	3	4	6	3	5	7	3	4	8	6
Catalogue from travel organizer/ company	11	2	15	10	10	14	12	11	11	12	8	8
Travel description in newspaper/ periodical/magazine	6	3	8	6	6	5	7	7	4	6	6	5
Advertisement/publicity in newspaper/ magazine	5	5	5	6	5	5	6	4	6	5	5	6
Radio/TV transmission	1	0	2	2	1	2	1	1	2	2	1	1
Guide books/travel books	9	4	12	9	10	9	11	9	7	9	8	11
No sources of information/knew beforehand	36	51	28	29	41	36	39	35	34	35	40	37
Other places	2	2	2	3	1	1	1	2	3	3	2	1
Total	130	112	139	134	129	128	134	129	125	130	125	129
Number asked	2,686	931	1,755	749	1,058	634	1,070	532	696	1,785	440	644
Total number (thousand)	2,759	956	1,803	769	1,087	651	1,099	547	715	1,834	452	662

The question was: 'Which sources of information have you used to choose the target for the most important holiday trip in 1990?'

Source: Danish Travel Analysis, 1991

11

International Tourism Marketing
Adapting the growth-share matrix

Josef A. Mazanec

The theme of this case is the strategic evaluation of a portfolio of products utilizing formal portfolio analysis. The viewpoint is that of the management of a National Tourist Office (NTO) in charge of promoting a tourist-receiving country. A number of countries or 'markets' become the objects to be evaluated in the portfolio, which looks at each individual tourism-generating country, its particular size of tourist demand, its growth rate and the market share attracted by the destination selected.

In 1990 the number of international tourist arrivals worldwide exceeded 400 million, and, according to the World Tourism Organization, tourist receipts amounted to more than US $250 billion. Roughly 60% of all tourist arrivals worldwide are recorded in Europe; the Americas, for example, only account for about 20%. Germany is the leading country in terms of international tourism generated per capita, and Austria is the world champion in terms of tourist receipts per capita.

The case situation is as follows. It is assumed that a new general manager has been appointed at the National Tourist Office (NTO) of the following European countries: Germany, France, Greece, the UK, Italy, Austria, Switzerland, Spain. She intends to introduce advanced methods of strategic planning. Hitherto such methods have not commonly been used in the NTO business of promoting tourist flows into a receiving country.

Strategic planning in an NTO entails one crucial decision to be taken at regular intervals (seasonally or annually). As a destination's portfolio consists of a mixture of travellers from various generating countries, management has to decide on how such marketing effort should be directed towards each of these markets. The NTO incurs the cost of market operation (with advertising consuming the bulk of the budget), but – as a non-profit organization – expects no direct financial response.

The tourist receipts will flow into the tourist industry, and the organization's performance is not measured in terms of revenue and profit. However, if one is prepared to substitute 'bed-nights sold' for the general concept of 'unit sales', the portfolio becomes manageable.

In addressing this key decision, the general manager wants to start with an analysis of the current situation. She proposes to utilize portfolio analysis to assist her to identify:

- the most significant tourism-*generating* countries as *markets*;
- the relative market shares and strengths of tourist-receiving countries as competitors;

Once these have been identified, she can go on to consider:

- which would be this NTO's key target markets and the proportion of promotional budget these should receive.

Portfolio analysis applied to tourist-receiving countries

The most widely used methods of strategic evaluation techniques are *portfolio models*, where a company is viewed as a portfolio of individual businesses or products and brands. The simplest model of the *growth-share matrix* employs three assessment criteria for products:

- market growth rate;
- relative market share (compared to the toughest competitor); and
- contribution to overall sales (importance value).

Obviously, an application to NTO management must account for the difference that NTOs spend budgets on advertising and promotion, but they do not sell tourist products themselves. Market share, however, is used in portfolio models as a proxy for relative profit performance, and the derivation of recommended strategies relies on this correlation.

In this context the strategic market positions of tourist-receiving countries can be evaluated with a set of assessment criteria as follows:

- The *market growth rate* is the percentage of the *relevant market volume*, where the relevant market volume comprises the total number of bed-nights sold by the nine major European receiving countries to the nineteen leading generating countries in the world during one calendar year.
- The *relative market share* is defined as a ratio of two market shares. The enumerator is the share of bed-nights sold by one particular receiving country in the bed-night total bought by a generating country. The denominator is the share of bed-nights attained by the biggest competitor. Thus, a relative share of 1.1 for a receiving country in a generating country X means that this country is the

market leader in X and excels the second-best competing destination by ten percentage points.

- The *importance value* is defined as the proportion of bed-nights sold to a particular generating country in the bed-night total of guests recorded in a receiving country. An importance value of, say, 10% for the generating country Netherlands in the receiving country Austria means that travellers from the Netherlands contribute 10% to the bed-night total produced by guests from abroad in Austria.

In a pictorial representation these evaluation criteria are portrayed along the vertical axis (growth rate) and the horizontal axis (relative share) and through the diameter of circles (importance values) for each major generating country. Exhibits 1 and 2 show an example for the former Yugoslavia as a receiving country and for nine generating countries in Europe – West Germany, the Netherlands, the UK, France, Belgium and Luxembourg (counted as one country), Italy, Sweden, Denmark and Austria – plus the USA. Management may then use the analysis to address questions such as:

- Which receiving countries were successful in tackling the growth markets?
- Is the portfolio rather one-sided or reasonably diversified? A single dominant circle indicates an unbalanced mixture of guest nations.
- Which receiving country has a dominant position in a generating market? Market dominance may reveal a competitive advantage by achieving economies of scale in market operation.

Data base and PC assistance

The NTO's market research department operates an up-to-date PC-aided market information system (MIS). You are provided with the international tourism data retrieved from the MIS in standard format (Appendix 1). The necessary transformations for portfolio purposes still have to be applied to derive the evaluation criteria. Spreadsheet calculations will facilitate this working step. If you are supplied with the special software support for this case (cf. Appendix 2), you receive some data files and a Windows program for producing the portfolio diagrams.

Exhibit 1   *Portfolio of Yugoslavia in 1989*

Generating country	Austria	Belgium/ Luxembourg	Denmark	France	Germany (FR)	Italy	Netherlands	Sweden	UK	USA
Market volume, 1989 (million bed-nights)[1]	20.3	38.2	13.3	47.9	229.6	48.3	50.2	14.5	100.0	59.0
Volume increase in 1988–9 (%)	0.5	6.1	−2.2	4.8	−1.3	7.8	0.4	3.6	−6.7	6.1
Yugoslavia's market share, 1989 (%)	22.2	3.1	3.8	2.3	7.6	12.6	7.0	4.8	5.9	1.0
Yugoslavia's relative share[2] (Toughest competitor)	0.65 (Italy)	0.07 (France)	0.14 (France)	0.07 (United Kingdom)	0.29 (Austria)	0.35 (France)	0.34 (France)	0.21 (United Kingdom)	0.13 (Spain)	0.02 (United Kingdom)
Importance value (%)[3]	9.1	2.4	1.0	2.2	35.6	12.4	7.1	1.4	12.0	1.2

[1] Comprises bed-nights in the 9 major receiving countries: Austria, France, Germany (FR), Greece, Italy, Spain, Sweden, UK, Yugoslavia (domestic tourism excluded).

[2] Compared to strongest competitor (parentheses).

[3] Percentage contribution to total bed-nights recorded in Yugoslavia (corresponds to diameter of circles in portfolio plots, Exhibit 2).

Source: TourMis Marketing Information System of the Austrian National Tourist Office

Exhibit 2   *Portfolio for Yugoslavia, 1989*

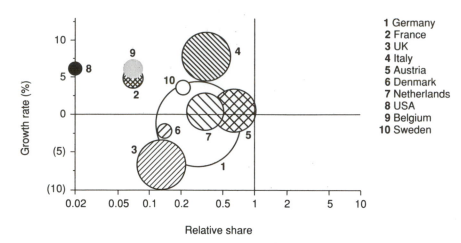

Questions for discussion/suggested tasks

1   Select any receiving country you feel familiar with. Sort out eight to ten tourism-generating countries which seem to be of crucial importance for this destination. Perform the necessary calculations and produce a portfolio plot. Write a report with your analysis, interpretation and recommendations for your country's NTO management. Comparison with at least one more competing destination will increase the strategic output.

2   There are ways to improve the type of strategic assessment you have applied. Be critical and give a brief summary of the strengths and weaknesses of the growth-share approach employed in this analysis. What other data, qualitative or quantitative, would you require to improve your strategic assessment of the attractiveness of generating countries and of the competitive positions of receiving countries?

Appendix 1: Data

Data are delivered as time series for the period 1980–9. Some adjustments required to render international bed-night figures comparable have already been made. The following collection contains a summary table of the relevant market volume of nineteen generators (Table 1), then an overview of the bed-night totals recorded in the nine leading European destinations (Table 2) and then one table with a breakdown of bed-nights by country of origin for each of these destinations (Tables 3–11).

Table 1 Market volume in Europe generated by each of nineteen countries of origin, 1980–9 (000 bed-nights)

Country	1980	1981	1982	1983	1984	1985	1986	1987	1988	1989
Australia/New Zealand	16,964	13,528	12,921	14,420	17,025	17,913	16,624	18,682	17,733	17,891
Austria	18,352	17,792	17,793	18,175	19,018	19,338	19,764	20,339	20,155	20,316
Belgium/Luxembourg	38,119	38,749	35,364	33,156	33,679	32,426	33,173	34,734	36,012	38,158
Canada	8,826	10,088	10,401	11,854	12,991	14,510	12,975	12,522	13,047	12,911
Denmark	9,208	9,533	9,501	10,110	10,464	12,144	13,713	14,365	13,586	13,253
Finland	3,149	3,372	4,279	3,361	5,153	4,724	4,511	5,834	5,643	6,475
France	40,230	39,845	42,226	38,855	43,161	42,401	42,727	48,701	45,690	47,888
Germany (FR)	221,752	223,255	220,604	217,034	215,572	218,330	224,555	230,797	232,609	229,620
Greece	2,693	2,433	3,045	2,728	2,872	3,172	2,786	3,488	3,605	3,467
Italy	25,085	24,308	25,185	28,860	33,232	35,981	36,264	42,958	44,825	48,311
Japan	5,236	5,621	5,737	5,741	6,432	7,655	7,131	8,874	10,120	11,392
Netherlands	50,687	49,214	47,416	45,224	46,789	47,258	49,311	49,123	49,984	50,203
Norway	4,698	5,175	5,663	5,810	6,097	7,945	7,446	6,374	5,665	5,671
Spain	11,566	11,078	11,325	12,033	12,038	13,748	16,075	17,737	19,305	20,780
Sweden	12,985	13,041	13,170	11,215	13,470	13,794	13,893	13,782	13,999	14,456
Switzerland	22,656	22,508	22,769	23,799	23,846	25,354	24,756	25,520	26,847	26,407
United Kingdom	73,002	85,633	93,368	97,184	106,660	91,467	111,486	112,534	107,235	100,039
United States	39,635	39,715	42,820	53,846	63,709	70,891	50,649	59,734	55,550	59,031
Yugoslavia	2,866	2,883	3,581	2,686	2,170	2,073	2,447	3,167	2,673	2,673
Sum foreign	687,948	701,134	704,802	711,829	751,944	767,139	777,158	818,414	836,271	850,442
Total relative change (%)	−1.3	1.9	0.5	1.0	5.6	2.0	1.3	5.3	2.2	1.7

Source: MIS calculations

Table 2 *Bed-nights sold by each of nine receiving countries (excluding domestic tourism), 1981–9 (000s)*

Country	1981	1982	1983	1984	1985	1986	1987	1988	1989
Austria	92,250.2	89,954.0	87,444.5	86,713.3	85,075.9	85,393.3	85,692.0	87,575.1	94,968
France	116,360.5	110,268.9	113,569.1	118,053.4	121,597.0	122,609.3	125,185.6	152,901.1	168,191
Germany (FR)	27,941.3	27,469.6	28,154.0	32,049.2	34,094.3	33,807.1	35,008.7	36,724.9	40,510
Greece	30,623.1	30,011.0	26,245.8	30,336.1	35,709.9	35,450.6	35,755.3	34,779.1	34,779
Italy	92,383.5	100,759.1	97,248.8	95,144.3	96,138.4	99,138.2	106,493.7	107,030.1	100,608
Spain	126,518.5	137,265.9	142,403.0	157,924.2	140,866.6	156,262.8	165,357.2	157,564.1	141,217
Switzerland	39,192.6	36,738.3	35,977.3	34,958.0	35,182.4	34,928.6	34,581.0	34,446.9	35,946
United Kingdom	135,900.0	136,755.0	145,432.0	154,496.0	167,659.0	158,169.0	178,244.0	172,899.0	185,044
Yugoslavia	39,694.6	35,580.4	35,354.9	42,269.8	50,815.8	51,399.5	52,299.1	52,351.0	49,175
Total	701,134.1	704,802.3	711,829.4	751,944.4	767,139.2	777,158.4	818,616.6	836,271.4	850,441
Total relative change (%)	1.9	0.5	1.0	5.6	2.0	1.3	5.3	2.2	1.7

Sources: OECD Statistics, Paris/World Tourism Organization, Madrid; Östat (Austrian Statistics Office)

Table 3 Bed-nights sold for Austria, by country of origin, 1980–9 (000s)

Country	1980	1981	1982	1983	1984	1985	1986	1987	1988	1989
Australia/New Zealand	148	139	146	150	178	193	171	185	188	238
Belgium/Luxembourg	2,826	2,979	2,585	2,317	2,347	2,245	2,163	2,259	2,348	2,657
Canada	142	151	169	177	210	246	210	227	223	221
Denmark	777	788	850	797	803	859	907	970	952	1,015
Finland	74	86	111	123	140	142	154	199	207	227
France	1,610	1,920	2,151	1,835	2,362	2,479	2703	2,666	2,652	2,897
Germany (FR)	65,579	65,989	62,727	60,464	57,407	55,432	56,055	54,937	56,059	59,922
Greece	106	114	117	119	136	138	123	162	174	189
Italy	703	831	929	1,051	1,246	1,264	1,519	1,691	2,091	2,787
Japan	127	156	166	182	198	234	230	308	321	371
Netherlands	9,768	10,338	9,724	9,047	9,354	9,177	9,176	9,320	9,269	9,659
Norway	87	95	117	132	144	176	206	228	207	195
Spain	158	156	157	185	182	211	215	286	365	456
Sweden	1,044	1,158	1,296	1,140	1,150	1,245	1,351	1,453	1,375	1,417
Switzerland	1,320	1,379	1,455	1,610	1,762	1,876	1,998	2,234	2,491	2,941
United Kingdom	2,208	2,682	3,559	4,060	4,339	4,233	4,298	4,250	4,213	4,720
United States	1,333	1,170	1,439	1,741	2,203	2,377	1,409	1,720	1,592	1,698
Yugoslavia	415	443	428	260	271	287	329	370	383	409
Sum foreign	90,203	92,520	89,954	87,444	86,713	85,076	85,393	85,692	87,575	94,969
Total relative change (%)	6.3	2.6	-2.8	-2.8	-0.8	-1.9	0.4	0.3	2.2	8.4

Source: Östat (Austrian Statistics Office)

Table 4 *Bed-nights sold for France, by country of origin, 1980–9 (000s)*

Country	1980	1981	1982	1983	1984	1985	1986	1987	1988	1989
Australia/New Zealand	806	766	766	900	792	888	783	760	750	825
Austria	1,264	1,384	1,279	1,217	1,242	1,023	979	837	849	934
Belgium/Luxembourg	17,609	18,010	16,712	15,582	16,027	15,242	15,271	14,860	15,012	16,154
Canada	1,062	1,526	1,171	1,405	1,771	2,191	1,938	1,872	1,873	2,061
Denmark	1,245	1,612	1,728	2,018	2,568	2,684	3,174	3,090	3,141	3,455
Finland	430	589	438	402	569	458	466	556	561	617
Germany (FR)	23,075	23,688	22,907	22,149	22,521	23,315	23,312	23,935	24,473	26,920
Greece	0	0	0	0	0	0	0	0	0	0
Italy	10,144	9,038	9,428	10,098	11,309	11,571	12,923	14,880	15,744	17,318
Japan	1,748	1,748	1,824	1,824	1,824	1,879	1,869	2,138	2,297	2,527
Netherlands	9,424	8,074	9,507	9,329	9,516	8,878	9,812	9,823	9,479	10,427
Norway	639	874	579	695	673	770	769	607	596	655
Spain	5,509	5,131	5,137	4,840	5,421	5,801	6,190	7,239	7,603	8,364
Sweden	1,826	2,269	1,347	1,341	1,487	1,336	1,435	1,313	1,400	1,540
Switzerland	5,337	4,973	5,283	5,340	5,736	5,793	5,460	5,291	5,261	5,787
United Kingdom	19,323	20,217	18,765	19,366	18,619	19,753	21,817	22,562	23,349	25,683
United States	5,857	6,743	6,620	10,005	12,006	13,603	10,202	11,203	11,564	12,720
Yugoslavia	0	0	0	0	0	0	0	0	0	0
Sum foreign	112,185	116,360	110,269	113,569	118,053	121,597	122,609	125,186	152,901	168,191
Total relative change (%)	0.9	3.7	-5.2	3.0	3.9	3.0	0.8	2.1	22.1	10.0

Sources: OECD Statistics, Paris/World Tourism Organization, Madrid

Table 5 Bed-nights sold for Germany, by country of origin, 1980–9 (000s)

Country	1980	1981	1982	1983	1984	1985	1986	1987	1988	1989
Australia/New Zealand	243	222	226	208	303	329	304	281	290	350
Austria	1,017	1,070	1,027	1,083	1,044	1,101	1,144	1,200	1,268	1,374
Belgium/Luxembourg	1,592	1,475	1,234	1,188	1,270	1,331	1,422	1,464	1,542	1,696
Canada	273	275	291	322	429	462	413	394	428	488
Denmark	1,189	1,321	1,273	1,241	1,367	1,492	1,649	1,603	1,657	1,694
Finland	190	221	217	234	261	292	318	330	370	427
France	1,545	1,570	1,483	1,279	1,483	1,571	1,635	1,681	1,789	2,000
Greece	218	234	240	235	237	255	254	271	322	352
Italy	975	1,060	1,121	1,159	1,223	1,285	1,416	1,501	1,724	2,009
Japan	668	792	835	840	885	1,036	1,056	1,176	1,286	1,526
Netherlands	6,632	6,053	5,824	5,831	6,108	6,016	6,486	6,788	6,939	7,195
Norway	307	375	401	422	419	532	642	587	587	640
Spain	346	408	403	366	412	460	501	553	654	749
Sweden	892	973	992	940	1,083	1,180	1,371	1,404	1,581	1,809
Switzerland	1,198	1,193	1,260	1,296	1,350	1,428	1,519	1,574	1,665	1,826
United Kingdom	2,715	2,560	2,554	2,569	2,892	3,011	3,133	3,065	3,120	3,575
United States	3,511	3,234	3,724	4,598	5,763	6,183	4,614	5,138	4,725	5,104
Yugoslavia	479	467	396	337	342	378	418	462	514	599
Sum foreign	27,916	27,941	27,470	28,154	32,049	34,094	33,807	35,009	36,725	40,510
Total relative change (%)	9.2	0.1	-1.7	2.5	13.8	6.4	-0.8	3.6	4.9	10.3

Sources: OECD Statistics, Paris/World Tourism Organization, Madrid

Table 6   *Bed-nights sold for Greece, by country of origin, 1980–9 (000s)*

Country	1980	1981	1982	1983	1984	1985	1986	1987	1988	1989
Australia/New Zealand	300	274	233	225	263	362	297	324	277	277
Austria	1,261	1,221	1,197	1,624	1,978	1,557	1,691	1,685	1,942	1,942
Belgium/Luxembourg	723	742	603	720	724	725	705	738	826	826
Canada	258	229	226	252	286	373	202	235	241	241
Denmark	794	837	939	943	787	1,090	1,305	1,337	1,214	1,214
Finland	461	528	532	508	736	1,112	1,235	1,311	1,345	1,345
France	2,390	2,352	2,660	2,378	3,223	2,797	2,581	2,730	2,594	2,594
Germany (FR)	6,405	6,123	5,933	7,132	8,459	7,357	7,593	7,715	8,316	8,316
Italy	1,103	1,103	1,096	1,603	1,608	1,573	1,517	1,757	1,793	1,793
Japan	211	207	206	225	238	257	208	239	262	262
Netherlands	1,229	1,262	1,033	1,142	1,433	2,004	2,061	1,757	1,752	1,752
Norway	615	634	873	864	705	1,076	1,101	1,014	724	724
Spain	161	155	134	154	184	223	237	283	321	321
Sweden	2,146	2,188	2,327	1,649	1,688	1,649	1,647	1,704	1,704	1,704
Switzerland	1,077	1,081	1,123	1,310	1,183	1,331	1,153	982	979	979
United Kingdom	5,938	7,275	7,711	6,701	7,864	7,630	8,692	8,308	7,285	7,285
United States	1,408	1,336	1,386	1,694	1,976	1,683	522	799	836	836
Yugoslavia	623	821	702	701	343	344	453	431	272	272
Sum foreign	29,520	30,623	30,011	26,246	30,336	35,710	35,451	35,775	34,779	34,779
Total relative change (%)	2.4	3.7	-2.0	-12.5	15.6	17.7	-0.7	0.9	-2.7	0.0

Sources: OECD Statistics, Paris/World Tourism Organization, Madrid

Table 7 Bed-nights sold for Italy, by country of origin, 1980–9 (000s)

Country	1980	1981	1982	1983	1984	1985	1986	1987	1988	1989
Australia/New Zealand	729	633	701	753	881	931	740	731	703	661
Austria	7,814	6,801	7,325	7,521	7,139	6,833	7,099	7,623	7,372	6,930
Belgium/Luxembourg	4,225	3,701	3,671	2,978	2,562	2,631	2,908	2,972	3,157	2,968
Canada	574	532	617	674	734	810	655	753	731	688
Denmark	1,158	953	1,041	941	892	1,041	1,296	1,451	1,473	1,385
Finland	428	364	438	553	537	575	610	765	733	689
France	8,047	7,470	8,413	6,737	7,013	7,234	7,595	7,813	7,468	7,020
Germany (FR)	45,377	39,745	43,802	42,705	41,353	41,754	44,725	47,571	48,047	45,164
Greece	546	569	671	592	771	562	504	507	529	497
Japan	493	520	587	619	635	629	711	997	1,214	1,141
Netherlands	5,402	4,265	4,340	3,562	3,082	3,321	3,659	3,795	3,956	3,718
Norway	323	351	425	448	420	507	599	568	492	463
Spain	1,008	1,000	1,129	1,127	1,182	1,292	1,387	1,685	1,935	1,819
Sweden	1,485	1,287	1,434	1,156	1,181	1,231	1,427	1,627	1,648	1,549
Switzerland	5,861	5,505	6,068	6,146	6,123	6,303	6,593	6,809	7,079	6,654
United Kingdom	7,483	6,666	7,179	7,220	6,220	5,992	7,124	7,067	6,584	6,189
United States	4,417	4,182	4,949	6,036	6,927	7,349	4,032	5,507	5,315	4,996
Yugoslavia	743	656	666	496	488	462	510	557	572	538
Sum foreign	103,282	92,383	100,759	97,249	95,144	96,138	99,138	106,494	107,030	100,608
Total relative change (%)	1.3	−10.6	9.1	−3.5	−2.2	1.0	3.1	7.4	0.5	−6.0

Sources: OECD Statistics, Paris/World Tourism Organization, Madrid

Marketing in Europe: case studies

Table 8 Bed-nights sold for Spain, by country of origin, 1980–9 (000s)

Country	1980	1981	1982	1983	1984	1985	1986	1987	1988	1989
Australia/New Zealand	452	434	399	332	360	370	347	343	342	362
Austria	1,180	1,479	1,591	1,549	1,665	1,832	1,758	1,918	1,909	2,081
Belgium/Luxembourg	4,581	5,668	5,526	5,427	5,729	5,258	5,850	7,467	7,641	7,413
Canada	345	480	500	609	706	828	587	389	313	305
Denmark	1,797	1,833	1,843	1,737	1,694	1,823	1,597	2,760	2,232	1,910
Finland	587	559	691	720	828	977	855	1,104	1,377	1,509
France	10,665	11,748	12,100	11,673	12,039	11,477	11,897	13,132	13,426	13,498
Germany (FR)	32,495	37,273	38,720	40,027	41,083	41,989	41,987	46,504	43,893	39,049
Greece	224	224	271	231	244	265	245	286	383	180
Italy	1,970	2,576	3,270	4,206	6,269	7,132	6,793	7,505	8,080	8,314
Japan	435	528	524	533	576	664	717	1,004	1,087	1,457
Netherlands	5,774	6,980	7,079	6,618	7,501	6,692	7,661	6,624	6,448	5,659
Norway	894	1,000	1,222	1,229	1,434	1,497	1,302	878	753	535
Sweden	2,115	2,209	2,477	2,040	2,226	2,214	1,933	2,062	2,119	2,102
Switzerland	2,767	3,300	3,162	3,583	3,824	3,681	4,028	4,375	4,248	3,935
United Kingdom	31,307	41,106	48,264	51,705	60,420	43,151	58,195	58,558	54,255	44,100
United States	2,453	2,729	2,842	3,571	4,232	4,347	2,553	3,274	3,011	3,146
Yugoslavia	193	177	183	155	149	150	195	236	194	223
Sum foreign	105,738	126,519	137,266	142,403	157,924	140,867	156,263	165,357	157,564	141,218
Total relative change (%)	−16.2	19.7	8.5	3.7	10.9	−10.8	10.9	5.8	−4.7	−10.4

Sources: OECD Statistics, Paris/World Tourism Organization, Madrid

Table 9 Bed-nights sold for Switzerland, by country of origin, 1980–9 (000s)

Country	1980	1981	1982	1983	1984	1985	1986	1987	1988	1989
Australia/New Zealand	286	261	269	284	325	360	315	283	266	310
Austria	546	563	532	514	489	498	496	508	505	522
Belgium/Luxembourg	2,984	3,083	2,320	2,064	1,918	1,928	1,969	1,992	2,011	2,120
Canada	212	229	245	280	316	376	315	292	256	269
Denmark	193	210	180	189	182	179	199	199	196	175
Finland	71	93	982	89	998	109	102	106	101	106
France	2,775	3,039	2,901	2,438	2,496	2,508	2,664	2,607	2,495	2,498
Germany (FR)	16,361	17,539	15,993	15,727	14,406	14,486	14,764	14,436	14,806	15,096
Greece	129	144	161	151	160	158	150	134	133	144
Italy	996	1,130	1,137	1,140	1,205	1,228	1,322	1,409	1,521	1,748
Japan	425	442	468	504	517	538	562	652	679	814
Netherlands	4,008	4,357	3,686	3,350	2,961	2,777	3,058	2,978	2,963	3,102
Norway	85	89	103	86	84	99	111	104	89	89
Spain	383	429	407	377	399	400	444	453	514	640
Sweden	273	297	333	295	297	319	364	350	363	339
United Kingdom	1,872	2,467	2,668	2,808	2,735	2,734	2,902	2,668	2,570	2,606
United States	1,922	1,979	2,310	2,615	3,320	3,552	2,328	2,573	2,269	2,465
Yugoslavia	112	119	980	78	81	86	95	104	110	134
Sum foreign	36,026	39,193	36,738	35,977	34,958	35,182	34,929	34,581	34,447	35,947
Total relative change (%)	19.9	8.8	-6.3	-2.1	-2.8	0.6	-0.7	-1.0	-0.4	4.4

Sources: OECD Statistics, Paris/World Tourism Organization, Madrid

Table 10 Bed-nights sold for United Kingdom, by country of origin, 1980–9 (000s)

Country	1980	1981	1982	1983	1984	1985	1986	1987	1988	1989
Australia/New Zealand	14,000	10,800	10,181	11,568	13,923	14,414	13,595	15,706	14,844	14,789
Austria	1,300	1,100	1,006	888	1,178	1,213	1,397	1,378	1,195	2,017
Belgium/Luxembourg	3,000	2,400	2,127	2,272	2,307	2,144	2,095	2,090	2,363	2,756
Canada	5,900	6,600	7,118	8,064	8,434	9,113	8,557	8,234	8,855	8,537
Denmark	1,800	1,600	1,312	1,785	1,481	1,983	2,443	1,967	1,912	1,901
Finland	800	800	727	576	899	884	633	1,316	775	1,393
France	12,000	10,400	11,171	11,467	13,043	12,793	12,212	16,709	14,045	16,259
Germany (FR)	16,100	15,300	15,521	14,108	14,304	14,586	16,391	15,655	17,226	17,624
Greece	1,300	1,000	1,415	1,226	1,142	1,621	1,344	1,943	1,846	1,870
Italy	6,500	5,700	5,225	6,372	6,211	6,963	6,128	9,235	8,507	8,198
Japan	1,100	1,200	1,099	987	1,533	2,398	1,754	2,331	2,944	3,262
Netherlands	6,400	5,300	4,415	4,794	4,563	5,374	4,373	5,162	5,566	5,206
Norway	1,500	1,500	1,677	1,676	1,889	2,068	2,388	2,071	1,882	2,121
Spain	4,000	3,800	3,958	4,984	4,257	5,269	6,108	7,106	7,780	8,275
Sweden	2,800	2,300	2,612	2,346	3,930	4,049	3,658	3,089	2,981	3,286
Switzerland	4,200	4,200	3,698	3,891	3,249	4,320	3,416	3,659	4,592	3,801
United States	18,400	18,000	19,186	23,140	26,678	31,204	24,613	28,940	25,520	27,432
Yugoslavia	300	200	225	659	495	365	447	1,008	627	498
Sum foreign	146,100	135,900	136,755	145,432	154,496	167,659	158,169	178,244	172,899	185,044
Total relative change (%)	-5.5	-7.0	0.6	6.3	6.2	8.5	-5.7	12.7	-3.0	7.0

Sources: OECD Statistics, Paris/World Tourism Organization, Madrid

Table 11 *Bed-nights sold for Yugoslavia, by country of origin, 1980–9 (000s)*

Country	1980	1981	1982	1983	1984	1985	1986	1987	1988	1989
Australia/New Zealand	0	0	0	0	0	67	71	70	74	80
Austria	3,971	4,174	3,837	3,779	4,283	5,280	5,200	5,190	5,114	4,515
Belgium/Luxembourg	578	690	588	608	796	922	790	891	1,111	1,209
Canada	61	65	64	71	106	112	97	125	126	102
Denmark	255	378	335	460	690	993	1,143	988	809	505
Finland	107	131	144	156	186	176	138	146	173	161
France	1,198	1,347	1,347	1,047	1,500	1,542	1,441	1,363	1,222	1,123
Germany (FR)	16,360	17,598	15,001	14,723	16,040	19,410	19,727	20,043	19,790	17,530
Greece	170	148	170	173	182	174	167	185	217	236
Italy	2,694	2,869	2,979	3,231	4,161	4,966	4,645	4,981	5,366	6,144
Japan	28	28	27	27	26	20	25	30	31	33
Netherlands	2,050	2,586	1,809	1,549	2,270	2,898	3,026	2,875	3,612	3,486
Norway	248	255	265	258	329	331	328	316	335	249
Spain	0	0	0	0	0	92	99	132	133	156
Sweden	404	360	353	308	430	571	707	780	827	710
Switzerland	897	877	720	622	619	622	588	596	533	485
United Kingdom	2,157	2,661	2,668	2,755	3,571	4,963	5,325	6,057	5,860	5,879
United States	334	341	363	447	604	594	378	580	720	633
Sum foreign	36,978	39,695	35,580	35,355	42,270	50,816	51,400	52,299	52,351	49,176
Total relative change (%)	10.4	7.3	-10.4	-0.6	19.6	20.2	1.1	1.8	0.1	-6.1

Sources: OECD Statistics, Paris/World Tourism Organization, Madrid

Appendix 2: PC support

PC assistance may be obtained from your case-study administrator. It comprises the PORTFWIN program and sample data files for producing portfolio plots. Copy the files PORTFWIN.EXE, VBRUN200.DLL, README.1ST and AUST89, . . ., YUGO89 to your hard disk, switch to this directory and run the PORTFWIN program. The Help option of the program briefly explains the pull-down menus; file README.1ST contains this Help text.

For PC users familiar with Lotus 1-2-3 the case material also includes a 1-2-3 worksheet with the raw data for thirteen generating countries and seven destinations. You should use the file RAW.WK1 for completing spreadsheet calculations of relative shares, growth rates and importance values. Table 12 is a printout of this worksheet. Check the calculations for Yugoslavia, which has already been presented as a sample output in the three-factor bubble chart of Exhibit 2. The other destinations are left as an exercise.

Table 12　Lotus worksheet with raw data

gen country	A	B+Lux	CH	D	DK	E	F	I	Japan	NL	S	UK	USA	total	all 19
mrkt vol 88	20.2	36.0	26.8	232.6	13.6	19.3	45.7	44.8	10.1	50.0	14.0	107.2	55.6	675.9	836.3
mrkt vol 89	20.3	38.2	26.4	229.6	13.3	20.8	47.9	48.3	11.4	50.2	14.5	100.0	59.0	679.9	850.4
vol increase abs															
vol increase %															
nights 89 sold by															
A	0.5	2.7	2.9	59.9	1.0	0.5	2.9	2.8	0.4	9.7	1.4	4.7	1.7	90.6	95.0
CH	2.1	2.1		15.1	0.2	0.6	2.5	1.7	0.8	3.1	0.3	2.6	2.5	32.0	35.9
E	2.1	7.4	3.9	39.0	1.9		13.5	8.3	1.5	5.7	2.1	44.1	3.1	132.6	141.2
F	0.9	16.5	5.8	26.9	3.5	8.4		17.3	2.5	10.4	1.5	25.7	12.7	132.1	168.2
I	6.9	3.0	6.7	45.2	1.4	1.8	7.0		1.1	3.7	1.5	6.2	5.0	89.5	100.6
UK	2.0	2.8	3.8	17.6	1.9	8.3	16.3	8.2	3.3	5.2	3.3		27.4	100.1	185.0
YU	4.5	1.2	0.5	17.5	0.5	0.2	1.1	6.1	0.0	3.5	0.7	5.9	0.6	42.3	49.2
max (row8. . .,14)	6.9														
mrkt leader	I														

for AUSTRIA:
mrkt share %
rel share
imp value %

for FRANCE:
mrkt share %
rel share
imp value %

	A	B+Lux	CH	D	DK	E	F	I	Japan	NL	S	UK	USA	total	all 19
for ITALY:															
mrkt share %															
rel share															
imp value %															
for SPAIN:															
mrkt share %															
rel share															
imp value %															
for SWITZERLAND:															
mrkt share %															
rel share															
imp value %															
for UNITED KINGDOM:															
mrkt share %															
rel share															
imp value %															
for YUGOSLAVIA:															
mrkt share %	22.2	3.1	1.9	7.6	3.8	1.0	2.3	12.6	0.0	7.0	4.8	5.9	1.0		
rel share	0.65	0.07	0.07	0.29	0.14	0.02	0.07	0.35	0.00	0.34	0.21	0.13	0.02		
imp value %	9.1	2.4	1.0	35.6	1.0	0.4	2.2	12.4	0.0	7.1	1.4	12.0	1.2		
gen country	A	B+Lux	CH	D	DK	E	F	I	Japan	NL	S	UK	USA	total	all 19

Key: A Austria; B+Lux Belgium/Luxembourg; CH Switzerland; D West Germany; DK Denmark; E Spain; F France; I Italy; NL Netherlands; S Sweden; UK United Kingdom; USA United States; YU Yugoslavia